Bell & Bain
Dictionary of
Commercial English

Bell & Hyman Dictionary of Commercial English

Edited by Keith Henderson
Laurence Urdang Associates Ltd

Bell & Hyman
London

Published in 1983 by
BELL & HYMAN LIMITED
Denmark House
37–39 Queen Elizabeth Street
London SE1 2QB

First published in 1979 by
Evans Brothers Limited

© Laurence Urdang Associates Ltd 1979

All rights reserved. No part of this publication may
be reproduced, stored in a retrieval system, or
transmitted, in any form or by any means, electronic,
mechanical, photocopying, recording or otherwise,
without the prior permission of Bell & Hyman Limited.

ISBN 0 7135 1449 3

Printed in England by
Cox & Wyman Ltd, Reading

Foreword

This dictionary of commercial terms has been written for the foreign student with a limited knowledge of English who needs to be familiar with the vocabulary of the modern business world. But people working in offices or in any way involved in the business world will find it a clear and helpful source of reference.

The dictionary covers 3000 headwords and collocations or groups of words (e.g. free sample). There is a detailed explanation of all the most common terms in shipping, banking, insurance and computing in current use, as well as many colloquial terms which can cause difficulty. The emphasis has been on explaining the meaning of the word or phrase in a business context, thus grammatical information and any superfluous non-commercial definitions have been avoided. The defining vocabulary has been restricted to about 2000 common English words to cause as little difficulty as possible to the student with limited knowledge of English.

There are numerous cross-references marked by an asterisk and the user is often directed to another entry for the sake of comparison, further explanation or clarification. Common abbreviations are entered alongside the appropriate headword but they do not occur in the definitions. Where the abbreviation differs from the appropriate headword because of the alphabetical order, the abbreviation is entered in its correct alphabetical position and the user is referred to the relevant headword.

Both British and American measurements have been specified. Lexical differences between British and American English and also spelling when these can hinder comprehension are fully explained. Latin and foreign expressions in current usage in business English have also been included.

A

abacus, a simple type of calculator consisting of beads strung onto wires set in a frame. Still in use in some Eastern countries.

abandonment. See constructive total loss.

aboard (of passengers or cargoes), on a ship or aircraft.

above par (of a share or other security), having a market value above its *nominal value.

abscond, to run away, especially to avoid legal proceedings or after having committed a crime.

absenteeism, staying away from work without having such reasons as sickness, public holidays, etc. In some countries more work is lost through absenteeism than through strikes.

absolute bill of sale, a *bill of sale in which the ownership of the goods is transferred without any restrictions or conditions.

acceptance, 1. an agreement to accept an offer of goods on the same terms as the offer. **2.** the writing on a *bill of exchange signifying that the person on whom it is drawn accepts the order of the person who has drawn it.

acceptance credit, a way of paying for goods in international trade. For example, a bank in an exporting country may open an acceptance credit on behalf of a foreign importer: the exporter will then be paid by *bill of exchange drawn on this bank.

acceptance for honour. See acceptance supra protest.

acceptance supra protest (acceptance for honour), the acceptance of a protested *bill of exchange by a person who wishes to save the honour of either the drawer or the endorser.

accepting house, a financial company, usually a *merchant bank, that accepts *bills of exchange drawn on it by customers that it considers worthy of credit.

acceptor, the person on whom a *bill of exchange is drawn after he has accepted liability.

accident insurance, the class of insurance that deals with personal accidents, accidents to employees, motor accidents, burglary, and other types of accident against which insurance cover can be obtained.

accommodation bill, a *bill of exchange signed by a person (the accommodation party) as guarantor to help another person. The accommodation party becomes liable if the acceptor fails to pay. *Also called* windmill.

accommodation party. See accommodation bill.

account, 1. a record of all the credits and debits relating to a customer in the books of a company. **2.** See bank account. **3.** a client of a company.

accountancy, the profession of an *accountant.

accountant, 1. a person who is professionally qualified to prepare and audit a company's annual accounts. **2.** a person who is trained in book-keeping and the keeping of a company's books of account.

account day, the day on which

accounts have to be settled, especially accounts on a stock exchange.

account executive, a person, especially one in an advertising agency, who is responsible for looking after the needs of one or more clients.

accounting cost, the total outlay of money by a company for all purposes in a given period. *Compare* economic cost.

accounting period, the period for which a company makes up its accounts. Usually it is one year.

account payee, words written across a cheque, by the person who writes the cheque, to make sure that the money is paid into the account of the payee only.

account rendered, words that often appear on a *statement of account to indicate previous invoices that have already been sent to the customer.

accounts, 1. the *balance sheet and *profit and loss account of a company. 2. the plural of *account.

account sale, an account detailing the sales that an agent has made on behalf of his principal. It usually shows the amounts received by the agent and the agents commission.

accounts payable, accounts that a company has not yet settled and on which it therefore owes money.

accounts receivable, accounts that have not been paid to a company and on which it is therefore owed money.

accredited agent, an officially recognized agent of a person or a company.

accrued charges, charges for goods or services that a company has incurred but not shown in its accounts. For example, electricity charges may have been incurred in one year but not paid until the following year.

accrued interest, interest that has been earned but not paid or received.

accumulated depreciation, the total *depreciation on an asset as shown in the accounts of a company.

acre, a unit of area equal to 4840 square yards or 4046·9 square metres (0.4047 hectare).

Act for International Development, an act passed in the U.S. in 1961, setting up the *Agency for International Development* (AID) to administer overseas economic aid.

action for damages, a legal case in which a person or company sues another for compensation, usually as the result of a broken contract.

active market, a market in which there are sufficient buyers and sellers to enable regular transactions to be made.

active partner, a member of a *partnership who takes part in the daily activities of the firm. *Compare* sleeping partner.

active stocks, stocks or shares in which there have been frequent transactions over a particular period.

act of God, an unforeseeable and unpreventable act of nature. Contracts sometimes exclude liability from damages that arise from such an act.

act of war, an act that causes damage to the citizens or property of a nation as a result of the activities of the citizens of another nation with whom they are at war.

actuals, consignments of commodities that can be purchased for delivery immediately or in the near future, as opposed to *paper transactions in *futures.

actual total loss, the total loss of a ship or cargo. *Compare* constructive total loss.

actuary, a person whose job is to calculate insurance risks and premiums.

adding machine, a mechanical device for adding and subtracting. Adding machines have been largely replaced by electronic calculators.

addressee, a person or company to whom something is addressed.

adjourn, to postpone a meeting or a legal case until some time, which is usually specified, in the future.

adjustment, the process of settling an insurance claim.

adjustor, a person who is appointed by an insurance company or insurer to settle a claim.

administration expenses, the expenses incurred in running a business, such as the costs of book-keeping and accounting. *Compare* direct expenses.

administrator, 1. a person who organizes the running of a business or other organization. **2.** a person appointed by a court to distribute the property of someone who has died but has not appointed anyone to do this in his will.

ad valorem, according to value. Taxes, commissions, charges, etc., are ad valorem when they are calculated on the value of the goods involved rather than on their quantity or weight.

advance, a loan of money against a security or in advance of a payment that will become due at a later date.

advance freight, the cost of transporting goods, usually by sea, that is paid before they are actually transported.

adverse balance, a deficit in an account, especially in a country's *balance of payments.

advertising, the publication of information about goods or services in order to persuade people to buy them.

advertising agency, an organization that handles the advertising of its clients' products.

advertising medium, one of several means for bringing advertisements to the public notice. The *media* include newspapers, journals, radio and television, and roadside hoardings.

advice note, a document sent by a supplier of goods to a customer to inform him that the goods have been sent to him. It usually states the quality and quantity of the goods, how they are marked, and how they have been sent.

advise fate, a request by a collecting bank to a paying bank to inform them whether or not the paying bank's customer has sufficient money in his account to meet a particular cheque.

advocate, a person who is trained to represent a member of the public in a court of law. The term *advocate* is used in Scotland in preference to the English *barrister*.

affidavit, a sworn statement made in writing and witnessed by a person authorized to administer oaths. Affidavits are usually required as evidence in a court of law.

affiliated company, a company that is closely connected with another company, usually as a result of common ownership.

afloat goods, goods that are on the high seas. They may be sold and on their way to the buyer or unsold and awaiting a purchaser.

after date, words used in a *bill of exchange to indicate the number of days after the date of the bill on which it will become payable; e.g. *90 days after date, we promise to pay....*

after-hours dealing

after-hours dealing, transactions that take place between members of an official market or exchange, after normal closing hours.

after-sales service, repair or replacement facilities available to a customer after he has purchased a product.

after sight, words used in a *bill of exchange to indicate that it is payable after the *acceptor has written the date of acceptance on it.

agency, 1. a business, such as an advertising agency or employment agency, that offers a service. **2.** the business of an *agent.

agenda, a list of the business that is to be discussed at a meeting.

agent, a person or firm that has authority to act on behalf of another. Manufacturers appoint *overseas agents* to sell their products abroad. An *exclusive* or *sole agent* is the only person or firm entitled to sell a particular product in a particular area.

agent de change, French for a stockbroker or dealer in currency.

A.G.M., abbreviation for *annual general meeting.

agricultural bank, a bank that specializes in giving long-term loans to assist farmers.

AID, abbreviation for Agency for International Development. *See* Act for International Development.

aids to trade, the four services that assist traders: banking, insurance, transport, and advertising.

air consignment note, another name for an *air waybill.

air freight, 1. the transport of goods by air. **2.** the cost of transporting goods by air from one place to another. It is usually based on the price per kilogram or per 7000 cubic centimetres, whichever is the greater.

air letter, a single sheet of lightweight paper that is folded into an airmail letter.

air waybill, a document made out by a person who sends goods by air freight. It details the goods, the person to whom the goods are being sent, and the airports of dispatch and destination. *Also called* air consignment note.

allonge, a slip of paper attached to a *bill of exchange to provide extra room for endorsements when the back of the bill has been covered.

allotment, the number of shares in a public company allocated to an applicant for a *new issue.

allowances, the amounts that can be deducted from a person's income in assessing his liability for tax. Examples are marriage allowance, child allowance, and single person's allowance.

all-risk insurance, 1. a form of insurance that covers a person's personal possessions against loss or damage, often when they are anywhere in the world. **2.** a type of *cargo insurance that covers all types of marine risk as laid down by the Institute of London Underwriters.

alternate director, a person empowered to act as a director of a company in the absence of another (named) director.

amalgamation, the joining together of two businesses for their mutual benefit.

amortization, 1. the process of writing off the value of a fixed asset in the accounts of a business over the expected life of the asset. For example, if a company buys a machine the total cost is not charged against the profits for the year in which it was bought, but a proportion is charged against the profits for, say,

appropriation

five years if the machine is expected to last for five years. **2.** the payment of a debt by instalments.

amounts differ, the words written on a cheque or *bill of exchange by a bank if the amount written out is different from the amount written in figures.

analog computer, a type of computer in which numbers are represented by such physical quantities as voltage or resistance. *Compare* digital computer.

anchorage, the fee charged by certain ports and harbours for permitting a ship to anchor in them.

annual accounts, the *accounts of a business that are prepared each year.

annual general meeting (A.G.M.), a meeting of the members of a company at which the *accounts are approved, directors appointed, etc. In most countries such a meeting must be held every year.

annual report, a report of the activities of a company that is sent out to all its members every year. It usually contains a review of trading in the past year and the prospects for the coming year, as well as the company's *accounts.

annual return, a form that has to be made out by a company every year, stating the names of the members, its address, etc.

annuitant, a person who receives an *annuity.

annuity, a type of pension in which a company, usually an insurance company, pays a fixed sum at regular intervals to an investor (or his nominee, such as his wife) for the rest of his (or his nominee's) life. The investor pays the company for this annuity either in one lump sum or in instalments.

annuity certain, an *annuity that is paid for a fixed term, such as 10 years, rather than for life.

annulment, cancellation of a contract, usually of marriage.

ante-date, to date a document earlier than the actual date on which it was executed.

anti-trust laws, U.S. laws that ensure a free competitive market and prevent the creation of *monopolies that would harm the consumer. The British equivalent is the *Monopolies and Mergers Act.

applicant, 1. a person who applies for a job. **2.** a person who fills out an *application form.

application and allotment, a method of allocating a *new issue of shares in a company to members of the public. A person fills in an *application form and sends it to the company or its bank, usually with a cheque for the amount of money required to pay for the shares. If there are more applications than shares available (*oversubscribed issue*) shares are allotted to applicants on the basis of a ballot, in proportion to their application, or in some other fair way.

application form, a form on which members of the public apply to buy shares in a company. *See* application and allotment.

appreciation, an increase in the value of an asset with the passage of time.

apprentice, a person who works for an employer for a fixed period, usually at a low wage, in order to learn a trade or craft.

appropriation, 1. a document in which a seller of a commodity, such as cocoa or jute, identifies the actual consignment that he will ship to the buyer in fulfilment of his contract. **2.** allocation of the profits of a business to dividends, reserves, etc. **3.** allocation to a particular debt of sums of money paid to a person by a debtor.

arbitrage, buying commodities, securities, or currencies, in one market and selling them in a different market to take advantage of differences in price, etc., between the two markets.

arbitration, the practice of referring a dispute between two parties to a contract to one or more independent persons (arbitrators) for a decision. Being cheaper and quicker than a legal action, it is frequently used in commercial disputes. It is usual for each side in the dispute to appoint its own arbitrator; if the arbitrators fail to agree they appoint an umpire to give the final decision.

arbitrator, a person appointed to act as a judge in an *arbitration.

architect, a person trained to design and supervise the construction of buildings, bridges, etc.

Ariel, a computerized system that enables subscribers to deal with each other in securities, rather than trade through an established stock exchange.

arithmetic mean, an average obtained by adding together all the quantities to be averaged and dividing the sum by the number of quantities. *Compare* geometric mean.

arithmetic progression, a sequence of numbers in which each term is greater than the one that comes before it by a constant amount, e.g. 3, 6, 9, 12, 15. *Compare* geometric progression.

arrangement, a plan for paying outstanding debts that a person in financial difficulty puts to his creditors.

arrears, money that is owed but has not been paid.

articled clerk, a person training to be a solicitor or accountant who is attached to a firm of solicitors or accountants in order to gain practical experience.

articles of association, the rules and regulations that control the working of a company.

A shares, shares in a company that have all the same rights as the ordinary shares except the right to vote at shareholders meetings. *Also called* nonvoting shares.

assay, a test to determine the percentage of precious metal in an alloy, especially in a coin or in bullion.

assembly line, a consecutive line of machines and operators, each of which perform a particular operation on a product, such as a motor car, during the course of its manufacture. The incomplete product passes down the line, emerging at the end as a complete unit.

assented shares, shares whose owners have agreed to a change of ownership, as in a *take-over bid, or to some other change in rights or conditions of issue.

assessment, 1. a statement by the taxation authorities showing the tax due by a taxpayer. **2.** a statement showing the damages suffered by a person or firm as calculated by an insurance assessor or adjustor.

assessor, 1. a person who calculates the extent of the damages suffered by a person or firm for insurance purposes. **2.** a person who assesses a taxpayer's liability for tax.

asset, any property owned by a person or business for which a money value can be given.

asset value (per share), the value of a company as estimated by deducting all liabilities from the *book value and dividing the difference by the number of shares in the company.

assignment, the transfer of the rights and obligations of a contract, such as an insurance policy, from one person to another.

associated company, a company that has a close relationship with another company, especially one in which the first company owns at least 20% of the shares of the second company.

associated state, a state that is not a member of the Common Market but that has a preferential trade agreement with member states.

assurance, the form of insurance associated with an event that must occur, such as a death, rather than with an event that may or may not occur, such as an accident.

assured, the owner of a life assurance policy.

at best, an instruction given to a broker to buy or sell securities or commodities at the most advantageous price, i.e. to buy at the lowest possible price or to sell at the highest. *Compare* at limit.

at call (of money), borrowed money that must be repaid on demand.

at limit, an instruction given to a broker to buy securities or commodities at or below a specified price or to sell at or above a specified price. *Compare* at best.

at par (of a share or other security), having a market value equal to its *nominal value.

at sight, words used on a *bill of exchange to indicate that payment becomes due on presentation rather than on a stated date.

attachment, a court order instructing a person who owes money to another person, who in turn owes money to a court, to pay the money direct to the court. Thus a court may recover a fine direct from the fined person's employer.

attorney, 1. a person who holds a *power of attorney. **2.** *in the U.S.* a lawyer.

at warehouse, contract terms in which a buyer of goods is responsible for the cost of delivering them from the seller's warehouse and for the cost of loading the goods onto the transport vehicles. *Compare* ex warehouse.

auction, a method of selling goods in which a person (the auctioneer) offers them for sale in public and sells them to the highest bidder.

auctioneer, a person who conducts an auction.

audio-typist, a person trained to type letters, etc., that have been dictated into a recording machine. *Compare* copy typist, shorthand typist.

audit, an examination of the books of account of a business to ensure that the accounts are a true and fair record of the business's trading.

auditor, an accountant trained to carry out an *audit on the *accounts of a business.

auditor's report, a statement by a qualified auditor that forms part of a company's *accounts and certifies that they give a true and fair record of the company's affairs. If in the auditor's opinion they do not do so he must state why.

authority, permission given to a bank by a client to act on his behalf in certain specified matters.

authorized capital, the amount of capital for which a company may issue shares. If the company wishes to increase the number of shares issued it has to increase its authorized capital by a resolution at a general meeting.

authorized clerk, a clerk who is empowered to carry out transactions on behalf of his employer.

automation

automation, the use of automatic control techniques in industrial processes.

available earnings, the earnings of a company that are available for distribution to *ordinary shareholders. They consist of the annual profits less taxation and less dividends on *preference shares and *minority interest shares.

average, 1. a single value that represents the general tendency of a set of values. *Also called* mean. *See* arithmetic mean, geometric mean, weighted average. **2.** loss or damage, especially as used in the context of insurance. *See also* particular average, general average, with average.

average adjustor, a person trained to calculate *average claims, especially for marine insurance.

average bond, a document in which a person who removes a cargo from the port of discharge after a voyage states that he will contribute to any *general average claim.

average clause, a clause in an insurance policy stating that for goods insured at less than their market value, claims for a partial loss will be settled on the basis of the ratio of the insured value to the market value.

average cost, the total cost of manufacturing a number of products, divided by the number of products. *Also called* unit cost.

average fixed cost, the part of the *average cost of a product that is fixed and does not vary with output. It is equal to the total fixed cost divided by the number of units produced.

average variable cost, the part of the *average cost of a product that varies with output. It is equal to the total variable cost divided by the number of units produced.

averaging, the process of buying securities or commodities as their price falls in order to reduce the average purchase price of a holding.

avoirdupois, a system of units of weight in which a pound consists of 16 ounces and a hundredweight consists of 112 pounds (100 pounds in the U.S.). The system is being replaced by metric units.

award, the judgment delivered by a panel of arbitrators.

B

back-to-back credit. *See* countervailing credit.

bad debts, debts that are unlikely to be paid and that, for accounting purposes, are treated as losses or are shown separately in a company's accounts as a *reserve for bad debts.*

bailee, a person who has possession, but not ownership, of the goods of another with his consent.

bailment, the placing of goods into the possession, but not the ownership, of another person.

bailor, a person who is the rightful owner of goods, or has the right to possess goods, who places the goods into the possession, but not the ownership, of another person.

balanced budget, a government budget in which current government expenditure equals current government revenue.

balance of payments, the difference between national income and national expenditure taking into account the difference between capital inflows and outflows including intergovernmental loans.

balance of trade (**visible balance**), the difference between the total value of a country's exports and imports of visible items (i.e. tangible goods as opposed to services).

balance sheet, a statement of the assets and liabilities of a company at a particular date.

ballast, material used in place of, or in addition to, cargo to stabilize a ship that is carrying less than its full load of cargo.

bank, a commercial institution that accepts deposits of money from its clients and pays out sums of money when instructed to do so. Banks also lend money to their clients and negotiate commercial documents for them.

bank account, a record of all transactions kept by a bank for each of its clients. *See* budget account, current account, deposit account.

bank advance (**bank loan**), a loan made by a bank against a security. Interest is payable on the advance at an agreed rate. *See also* bank overdraft.

bank bill, a *bill of exchange issued or accepted by a bank.

bank charges, the interest and commission charged by a bank to a client's account, usually half-yearly.

bank deposit, 1. an amount of money placed by a customer in a bank *deposit account. **2.** an instrument of government monetary policy intended to control credit by obliging commercial banks to make special deposits with a central bank to restrict their lending.

bank draft, a cheque drawn on a bank by itself or its agent, payable on demand or at a specified future date.

banker, 1. a person who manages a bank or is in the banking business. **2.** a person who holds money for another or who lends him money.

banker's clearing house, an institution that enables member banks to exchange cheques simply and efficiently. Payments are made between banks at the end of each day.

banker's indemnity, a guarantee given

banker's order

by a bank to a ship-owner to enable the consignee of goods to obtain possession of goods without showing the *bill of lading.

banker's order (standing order), an instruction to a bank by a client to pay a certain sum (e.g. an insurance premium) at regular intervals.

banker's reference, a formal document giving the opinion of a bank as to a customer's trustworthiness for trade credit, etc.

bank giro. See credit transfer.

bank holidays, a weekday on which banks are closed by law, e.g. Christmas Day, Easter Monday.

bank notes, paper currency issued by the central bank of a country.

Bank of England, the central bank of the U.K., which has the right to issue *bank notes. The bank carries out the government's monetary policy and manages the national debt.

bank overdraft, a loan made by a bank not necessarily against a security. The client is allowed to overdraw his *current account and interest has to be paid on the amount overdrawn. See also bank advance.

bank rate, the official rate of interest charged by a central bank or the rate at which it will discount *bills of exchange. See also minimum lending rate.

bank reconciliation statement, a formal entry in a cash book to account for the difference between the balances shown in a bank statement of account and those shown in the cash book. It may be necessary because cheques or cash, issued or received, may not have been banked when the bank statement was issued.

bankruptcy, the judgment of a court that a person is insolvent and unable to pay his debts. This judgment may be sought by the person concerned or by his *creditors. A receiver is appointed of the bankrupt's property, which is then sold and the proceeds distributed amongst the creditors.

bank statement, a statement of client's account issued by a bank. It gives a record of all transactions in the period covered and shows the balance outstanding.

banque d'affaires, an investment bank that helps industries by buying their shares (especially new issues) and selling them to investors. In some countries this function is often carried out by the merchant banks.

bar chart (bar diagram), a graphic display of statistics to enable comparisons to be made. Various items are represented by vertical or horizontal bars, the length of which are proportional to the magnitude of the items they represent.

bargain, 1. a cheap offer of goods. 2. a transaction on a stock exchange.

barge, a flat-bottomed freight boat commonly used on canals, rivers, etc.

barratry, any wilful act by the captain or crew of a ship to cause damage to the ship or its cargo, including theft of cargo by the crew.

barrel, 1. a cask for transporting liquids. 2. a measure of liquid volume. In the brewing industry 1 barrel contains 36 Imperial gallons (31·5 gallons in the U.S.); in the oil industry 1 barrel contains 42 U.S. gallons (35 Imperial gallons).

barrister, the U.K. name for a lawyer who is qualified to plead or defend a case in court.

barter, to trade by exchange of goods, without the use of money.

base metal, a non-precious metal, such as copper, zinc, lead, and tin.

base period, the period with which an index number or growth rate is compared. The base period is usually given the index number 100. If the period is one year the base period is called the *base year.*

base rate, the basic rate of interest charged by a bank. Actual rates of interest charged may be higher than the base rate and depend upon the type of advance and the credit rating of the customer.

base year. *See* base period.

basic pay, the wages or salary of a person before deductions of tax, etc., or the addition of overtime payments.

bear, a person who believes that the price of a certain share or commodity will fall. If he believes this confidently enough he may sell that share or commodity without having bought it, in the hope that he will be able to buy it later and make a profit when the price has fallen. *See also* short selling. *Compare* bull.

bear closing, the buying back by a *bear of shares or commodities that he has sold short (*see* short selling).

bearer, the possessor of a *bill of exchange or cheque marked "pay bearer". If not crossed (*see* crossed cheque) such a bill or cheque may be cashed over the counter at the bank to which it is addressed, without endorsement.

bearer bonds, negotiable *securities, possession of which is regarded as proof of ownership. They may be freely transferred without registering the change with the company.

bearish, (of a trader in shares or commodities) believing that prices will fall. *Compare* bullish.

bear market, a market in which prices are falling, enabling *bears to cover their short sales (*see* short selling) profitably.

bear position, the state of a *bear who has engaged in *short selling and therefore has shares or commodities sold but nothing bought against these sales.

bear raid, the selling of shares or commodities in order to force the price down in the hope that the seller will be able to buy back the shares or commodities at a lower price.

below par, (of a share or other security) having a market value below its *nominal value.

beneficial interest, the right to use and benefit from a property and to take income produced by it, without being the legal owner. For example, the legal owners of a trust are the trustees, but the beneficiaries of the trust have a beneficial interest in it.

beneficial owner, a person who has a *beneficial interest in property and is entitled to all the benefits accruing from ownership.

beneficiary, a person who receives benefits, especially the income of a trust or the proceeds of an insurance policy.

benefit in kind, benefits other than money received by employees, e.g. a company car, cost-price purchases of goods, etc.

benefit taxation, the taxation of those who receive a benefit from a public service, e.g. locally raised rates or taxes to pay for local services.

Benelux, the group of countries Belgium, the Netherlands, and Luxembourg.

bid, the reply of a buyer to an *offer made by a seller. If a firm makes an offer to sell goods at a certain price on certain terms a buyer may make a bid at a lower price or demand more advantageous terms. The seller may accept the bid or make a *counteroffer.

bilateral trade agreements

bilateral trade agreements, trade agreements arranged by the respective governments of two countries to increase trade between them, to abolish *trade barriers for certain goods, etc.

bill broker, a buyer and seller of *bills of exchange or an intermediary in such activities.

bill in a set, a *bill of exchange issued in duplicate or triplicate. Payment of one discharges the whole. They are used for overseas trade, one set usually being sent by airmail and another by sea mail to reduce the risk of loss.

bill of entry, a form required by the U.K. Customs and Excise detailing goods that are to be imported into the U.K. It has to be presented at the port of entry to the U.K. to enable goods to enter the country.

bill of exchange, a written order from one person (the drawer) to another (the drawee) requiring the drawee to pay a specified sum on demand or on a specified date to the drawer or to a person specified by the drawer.

bill of lading, a document entitling a buyer of goods the right to claim them from a ship. The document is made out by the shipping company that owns the ship, two copies usually being sent to the buyer of the goods. The buyer obtains the goods by presenting his copy of the bill of lading to the ship's master. *See also* clean bill of lading, dirty bill of lading.

bill of quantities, a document prepared by a quantity surveyor detailing the labour and material required for the design and construction of a building.

bill of sale, a document used to transfer the title to goods to another person, absolutely or conditionally, possession remaining with the person making the transfer. The bill of sale must show the rate of interest, the date of repayment, and any other agreed conditions. It is used as a security when borrowing money.

bill of sight, a document submitted to the U.K. Customs and Excise by an importer if he is unable to give a full description of his goods until they are landed and inspected.

bill rate, the rate at which *bills of exchange will be discounted.

bills payable, 1. a list of the sums of money owed by a firm. **2.** *bills of exchange held and due for future payment by the holder.

bills receivable, 1. a list of the sums of money owed to a firm. **2.** *bills of exchange held and due for future payment to the holder.

binding agreement, an agreement between parties that they are under a moral and legal obligation to keep.

birth rate, the number of live births in a country per 1000 of the average population for that year.

black list, a list of persons under suspicion, disfavour, censure, etc., or a list of fraudulent or unreliable customers or firms.

black market, an illegal market that violates price controls or other regulations.

blank bill, a *bill of exchange in which the name of the payee is not stated.

blank cheque, a cheque that is signed by the drawer but on which no sum of money is stated.

blank endorsement, a *bill of exchange endorsed in blank, i.e. no endorsee being named, in which case the bill becomes payable to the bearer.

blanket policy, an insurance policy that covers many different types of risk.

bourse

blocked accounts, bank accounts, usually in a foreign country, from which money can not be sent abroad owing to currency restrictions.

blocked currency, currency that cannot be removed from a country for any reason.

blue chip, shares of well-known companies considered to be reliable and, therefore, a safe investment. *Compare* gilt-edged.

blue-collar worker, a manual worker who works on the shop floor. *Compare* white-collar worker.

board meeting, a meeting of the directors of a company.

board of directors, the directors of a company who are concerned with managing the company on behalf of the shareholders.

bond, a redeemable security carrying a fixed rate of interest, used for raising money by a government or a firm.

bonded goods, imported goods on which duty has not been paid and which have been placed in a *bonded warehouse.

bonded warehouse, a warehouse, usually at a port, in which imported goods can be stored pending payment of customs or excise duties or re-export.

bondholder, a holder of bonds issued by a government or company.

bond note, dutiable goods entering a country are usually put in bond by the customs authorities until any import duty has been paid. A bond note is then issued to indicate that the formalities have been completed and that the owner of the goods has authority to recover them from the *bonded warehouse.

bonus, 1. something given or paid over and above what is due. 2. a sum of money paid to a shareholder, partner, or employee over and above his regular dividend or pay.

bonus issue, a free issue of shares by a company to its existing shareholders as a result of *capitalization of reserves. A 1 for 5 bonus issue is one in which existing shareholders get one free share for every five that they hold.

book cost. *See* book value.

book debts, the debts that show as owing in the books of a company. Some may, however, be *bad debts and may never be recovered.

books of account, account books used to keep a record of a company's financial affairs on a day-to-day basis. They include a cash book, ledger, sales and purchase ledgers, day books, etc.

book value, the *written-down value of an asset as shown in the books of a company, i.e. the cost less the total depreciation. *Also called* book cost.

boom, a situation in which the economy of a country, or a part of it, is working at full capacity. It forms a part of the *trade cycle.

bottom, 1. the part of a ship that is under the water. 2. a ship, especially in the phrase *shipped in separate bottoms* (meaning 'shipped by different vessels').

bottomry bond, a security for a loan to a ship's master in need of money to complete a voyage. The security is the ship and its cargo.

bought note, a contract note issued by a stockbroker or commodity broker as legal evidence of a transaction in which he has bought shares or goods for his client's account. It gives the details of the purchase, commission, and date when payment is due.

bourse, the French name for a stock exchange.

boycott

boycott, to abstain from buying or using a product, sometimes as a means of intimidation or coercion.

branch banking, a system of banking in which a small number of banks have a great many branches.

branch office, the local office of a large company.

branded goods, goods packed and marked with a proprietary brand name.

brand leader, the most successful brand of a particular product. The policies of its manufacturer are likely to be copied by the manufacturers of less successful brands.

brand name, the name of a particular product or range of products that distinguishes the output of a particular manufacturer from that of other manufacturers in the same industry.

breach of contract, the breaking, by action or omission, of an obligation imposed by a contract.

break-even point, the point at which the total income from a project is equal to the total investment.

break-up value, the asset value per share of a business, calculated by deducting the total liabilities from the total assets and dividing the resulting sum by the number of ordinary shares issued.

bribe, 1. money, goods, or services given or promised for corrupt behaviour in the performance of official or public duty. **2.** something given to a person to persuade him to do something he would not otherwise do.

bribery, the act or practice of giving or accepting *bribes.

bridging-loan, a short-term loan to enable a borrower to complete a purchase before he receives funds from another source.

broker, an agent who buys or sells for a principal on a commission (brokerage) basis without having title to the goods or property in which he deals.

brokerage, the commission charged by a *broker.

B.S.I., the British Standards Institution, which seeks to improve, standardize, and simplify industrial materials and to set standards of quality. It also registers and licenses quality marks.

budget, a prediction of the financial behaviour of a business enterprise (or of a government's expenditure) over a specified period of time. It usually consists of a detailed analysis of anticipated costs compared with anticipated income.

budget account, a bank account that, by arrangement with a bank, can be used for regular payments of various commitments such as rates, insurance policy premiums, etc., as they fall due. The total commitment is charged, by monthly payments, to the customer's *current account.

budgetary control, a means of ensuring that the *budget of a firm or government can be regularly checked to ensure that predicted income and expenditure are in accordance with predictions. If they are not warning is given to enable appropriate action to be taken.

budgetary policy, government taxation and expenditure policy to regulate the economy of a country.

budget deficit, a deficit that occurs if a government's expenditure exceeds the revenue raised by taxation, etc.

budget surplus, a surplus that occurs if a government's revenue from taxation, etc., exceeds its expenditure.

buffer stock, a stock of a raw material held by a government to stabilize its

by-product

market price. The market is supported by further purchases when prices fall and depressed by sales from the buffer stock when prices rise.

building society, a company that invites investors to take shares in the company or to make deposits with it at a fixed rate of interest. The funds so obtained or lent on *mortgage, at a higher rate of interest, to people who wish to purchase property (usually their homes).

bulk cargo, a cargo that is all of one commodity and can thus be shipped in bulk container or directly in the hold of a ship, without being packed in bags, barrels, etc.

bulk carrier, a ship designated to carry a particular *bulk cargo, e.g. oil, grain, etc.

bull, a person who believes that the price of a certain share or commodity will rise. If he believes this confidently enough he may buy that share or commodity without having sold it, in the hope that he will be able to sell it later at a profit when the price has risen. *Compare* bear.

bullion, gold or silver in bars.

bullish, (of a trader in shares or commodities) believing that prices will rise. *Compare* bearish.

bull market, a market in which prices are rising.

bull position, the state of a *bull who has bought shares or commodities without selling them.

bunkering, the fuelling of a ship, usually with oil or coal.

burglary, the act of breaking in to homes, shops, offices, etc., by persons who intend to commit a felony.

business, 1. a person's occupation, profession or trade. **2.** the purchase or sale of goods for the purpose of making profit. **3.** an established trading enterprise or concern.

business cycle. *See* trade cycle.

business expenses, expenses incurred in the course of business, which can properly be regarded as chargeable to the costs of running the business and which, therefore, earn tax relief.

business hours, the times at which a business is open to the public.

business interruption policy. *See* consequential loss policy.

business reply service, a service provided by the postal authorities in some countries to enable firms, at an agreed cost, to issue reply-paid envelopes or cards to their customers.

buyer's market, a market in which supply exceeds demand and buyers, to some extent, are able to dictate the prices. *Compare* seller's market.

buyer's over, a situation in a market in which there are still buyers after the sellers have sold all that they are able or willing to sell.

buying in, the process of buying goods, shares, etc., on behalf of a supplier who has failed to deliver these goods, shares, etc., in default of his contract to do so. The defaulting supplier is charged with the difference between the price paid and the contract price and any incidental expenses.

by-product, a secondary or incidental product in a manufacturing process.

C

cable, 1. a rope or chain used to hold a vessel at anchor or at a wharf. **2.** a telegram sent by submarine cable.

C.A.D. *See* cash against document.

calculator, a device for carrying out mathematical calculations. Most calculators are now electronic.

calendar, 1. any of various systems of reckoning time, especially with reference to the beginning, length, and divisions of the year. **2.** a tabular arrangement of the days of each month in the year.

calendar year, a period of 365 days, on 366 days in a leap year, divided into 12 calendar months beginning on January 1st and ending on the following December 31st.

called-up capital, the portion of a *share's price that is payable when the share is first issued.

call money, money lent for a short period that must be repaid on demand.

call option, an *option to buy shares, commodities, etc., at their current price within a specified period. To buy such an option costs a specified sum of money, which is forfeited if the option is not taken up. Thus, if the price of the share or commodity rises by more than the cost of buying the option, the buyer will call for the shares or commodity and be able to resell them at a profit. *Compare* put option.

canal, an artificial waterway for navigation, drainage, irrigation, etc.

cancelled cheque, a cheque marked by a bank to indicate that the value has been paid to the payee, i.e. that the cheque is no longer valid or negotiable.

C & F. *See* cost and freight.

capital, 1. wealth in the form of money or property owned by or employed in a business. **2.** any form of wealth used in the production of more wealth or available to be used to produce more wealth.

capital account, 1. an account recording inflows and outflows of capital, both long-term and short-term, that together with the *current account of national income and expenditure, makes up the *balance of payments of a country. **2.** an account showing the owners' interests in the assets of a business.

capital (investment) allowance, a tax allowance made by certain governments to encourage companies to increase production by investing in new plant and machinery, etc.

capital asset. *See* fixed assets.

capital budget, a forecast of the capital requirements for the future developments of a firm. *Compare* operating budget.

capital commitments, *capital expenditure to which a firm is committed but has not yet paid. These commitments are shown in the firm's accounts.

capital expenditure, the purchase of *fixed assets for the purpose of increasing production.

capital gain (capital profit), increase in the monetary value of an asset. The gain may not be a real one if in the period between the purchase and sale of the asset money has depreciated in value through *inflation. *Compare* capital loss.

capital gains tax, a tax on the profit made from the sale of an asset.

capital gearing, the control of the relationship between *equity capital and other invested capital in a business. With *low gearing* a firm's capital is mainly derived from equities (ordinary shares) as opposed to *debentures, fixed-interest loans, and other debts; *high gearing* is the opposite.

capital goods, goods used to produce machinery, materials, equipment, etc., which are, in turn, used to produce *consumer goods.

capital-intensive industry, an industry in which the costs of purchasing and maintaining the necessary capital equipment are high in relation to the costs of the labour required to run the business. *Compare* labour-intensive industry.

capitalism, an economic system in which individuals and firms are free to own *capital and the means of production. They may also compete with each other in order to make a profit in meeting consumer demands for goods and services.

capitalization, 1. the amount of capital in a company calculated by adding together its share capital debentures, loan capital, and reserves. **2.** the market value of a company calculated by multiplying the number of shares issued by the current share value. **3.** the process of converting *capital reserves into shares.

capitalization issue, the conversion of *capital reserves into issued shares by means of a *scrip issue.

capitalized value, the notional value of an *asset calculated from the annual income derived from the asset.

capital levy, a tax on private capital rather than on income.

capital loss, a decrease in the monetary value of an asset. *Compare* capital gain.

capital market, the market dealing with the long-term *capital required for financing commerce and industry, government projects, etc.; the money is obtained from stock exchanges, large investment institutions, insurance companies, banks, etc.

capital movements, the movement of funds from one country to another by companies or individuals for investment or speculative purposes.

capital profit. *See* capital gain.

capital reserves, funds in a company that may not be distributed to shareholders except through a *capitalization issue.

capital stock, the total value of the *fixed assets of a company after deducting *depreciation.

capital structure, the composition of the long-term *capital reserves of a company.

capital transfer tax, a tax levied on capital when it is transferred from one person to another. It covers death duties (estate duties) and transfers of capital made as a gift (gifts tax).

capital turnover, the annual sales of a company divided by the capital invested in it.

carat, 1. a unit used to express the purity of gold. Pure gold is defined as 24 carat; the weight of gold in an alloy is expressed as the number of parts of pure gold in 24 parts of the alloy. E.g. 14 carat gold contains 14 parts of gold and 10 parts of some other metal (usually copper). **2.** a unit of weight for gemstones (especially diamonds) equal to 0·2 grams.

carbon copy

carbon copy, a duplicate copy made using *carbon paper.

carbon paper, paper faced on one side with wax containing a dye (often carbon black). It is placed between two sheets of plain paper to reproduce on the lower sheet whatever has been written or typed on the upper sheet.

cargo insurance, insurance covering the risks involved in shipping cargo. Whether the seller or the buyer pays for the insurance depends upon the conditions of sale. *See also* free of particular average, with average, war risk insurance.

carnet, an international customs document allowing temporary duty-free import of certain goods into certain countries.

carriage costs, when a seller of goods pays for the cost of delivering them to the buyer, the price of the goods will include the statement *carriage paid*, or *carriage free* if he is using his own delivery service. When the buyer has to pay for the cost of delivery the price is *carriage forward*.

carriage forward. *See* carriage costs.

carriage paid. *See* carriage costs.

carrier, 1. a *common carrier* is a person or firm whose transport is available to the general public to carry goods safely and securely at his risk, for a reasonable fee. 2. a *private carrier* offers the same service, not to the public generally, but on specific contracts.

carry-over, the surplus crop or quantity of a commodity left on the producer's hands at the end of a growing or producing season. When carried over to the following season and added to the anticipated yield of the new crop it will affect pricing structure. *See* supply and demand.

cartel, a monopolistic association of companies wishing to reduce competition between themselves in a market by agreeing to regulate prices or terms of sale.

carton, a cardboard or plastic container for goods.

case of need, an endorsement on a *bill of exchange that names a person to whom the holder may apply if the bill is not paid.

cash, money in the form of coins or paper notes, as opposed to cheques, etc.

cash against documents (C.A.D.), a method of paying for goods sold for export. The seller sends the shipping documents to a bank or agent at the port of destination, who present the documents to the buyer (usually before the goods are due to arrive). The buyer pays for the documents and can then obtain the consignment when it arrives by producing the documents as proof that he has paid for the goods. *Also called* documents against presentation.

cash book, an account book containing a record of all the receipts and payments made by a business.

cash box, a box, usually with a secure lock, in which cash is kept.

cash discount, a reduction in the price of goods, offered to ensure prompt payment.

cash dispenser, a device, usually installed in banks, enabling customers to use special cards to obtain cash from a slot-machine. All transactions are automatically recorded so that the customers' accounts can be charged accordingly.

cash flow, the amount of money received and paid by a firm. A *cash flow projection* is an estimate of anticipated receipts and payments for a specified period in the future.

cashier, 1. a person who receives and pays out cash. 2. a person who records entries in a firm's *cashbook.

cash on delivery (C.O.D.), a service enabling businesses to send parcels by post to customers, who then make payment to the postman on delivery.

cash price, the price of goods paid for at the moment of sale. *Compare* hire-purchase price.

cash ratio, the ratio of the amount of money kept in reserve by a bank to meet the needs of its customers to the total of the credit balances held on behalf of all its customers.

cash with order, payment terms for goods in which the buyer has to pay the seller when he places the order.

casting vote, the deciding vote cast by the chairman of a meeting, presiding officer, etc., when the voting is equally divided.

catalogue, a list, often in alphabetical order, giving details of the articles listed. It is often a list of articles for sale or of paintings in a gallery.

catalogue price, the price of goods listed in a *catalogue, which offers goods for sale.

census, an official counting of all the people in a country or district, to obtain details of age, sex, occupation, etc.

central bank, a bank that acts as banker to a government and works closely with the government to help to put its policy into action.

certificate, any document that certifies the truth of something, such as the status or qualifications of the holder or gives evidence as to his ownership of something.

certificate of incorporation, a statement showing that a company has been duly incorporated.

certificate of origin, a document showing the name of the country from which a shipment of goods has originated. This is needed to decide what import duties must be paid as rates vary according to agreements between countries.

certified accountant, a professional accountant who is qualified to prepare and audit annual accounts of companies, etc.

chain stores, shops that are owned by a large organization and are well-known in most towns throughout a country.

chairman, 1. the person who presides at a meeting. 2. the nominal head of a business who presides at meetings of the board of directors of a company.

chairman's report, an annual report on the activities of a company, or of any similar organization, made by a chairman at the *annual general meeting. It sets out the activities of the company during the preceding year and often gives a review of the company's activities in the coming year.

chamber of commerce, an association of local traders in towns and cities for the purpose of protecting their interests, providing information, etc. The International Chamber of Commerce, in Paris, exchanges information relating to international trade between local chambers of commerce.

chamber of shipping, an association of ship-owners and others connected with shipping for the purpose of protecting their interests.

chamber of trade, a central organization representing local *chambers of commerce on a national basis, designed to protect the interests of members in the distributive trades.

chandler, a dealer or trader, especially a supplier of stores to maritime vessels.

charge

charge, 1. the money to be paid in return for goods or services. 2. an entry in an account. 3. a security against loans made to a company. A *specific charge* is secured against a specified asset of the company, whereas a *floating charge* is secured over all the assets of the firm.

charges forward, a condition of sale stipulating that the delivery charges must be paid by the buyer when he receives the goods.

chartered accountant, a member of the Institute of Chartered Accountants. Chartered accountants tend to specialize in auditing accounts and preparing company balance sheets. *See also* certified accountant.

chartered company, a company created by royal charter in the U.K. Municipal and county boroughs are usually incorporated in this way.

chartering, the hiring of a whole vessel to carry goods, rather than hiring cargo space on a vessel that carries cargoes for other shippers. *Time charters* are arranged for a fixed period of time, whereas *voyage charters* are arranged for a fixed number of voyages.

chartering agent, an agent or broker who arranges the *chartering of ships.

charter party, the contract drawn up to control the *chartering of a ship.

chattels, movable items of property, as opposed to fixtures.

cheap money, money that can be borrowed at a low rate of interest. *Compare* dear money.

chemical engineer, an engineer qualified to design, manufacture, and operate plant or machinery used in industrial chemical processes.

cheque, a form of *bill of exchange that is drawn on a bank and is payable on demand. They are widely used for settling debts and for drawing money from a bank. A *crossed cheque can only be paid into a bank account.

cheque book, a book of blank *cheques issued by a bank for the use of a customer with an account at the bank.

cheque card, a card issued by a bank to a customer who has an account with the bank, to enable him to make purchases on credit or to cash cheques up to a specified limit. The bank acts as a guarantor up to this limit.

children's assurance, an insurance policy taken out by a parent on his or her life either: (a) to save money for the child until it reaches a certain age, when the proceeds may be taken or the child may continue the policy on its own behalf; (b) to provide an educational endowment.

chose in action, a right to property held by someone other than the possessor. The right is negotiable. Choses-in-action are usually mortgages, insurance policies, cheques, etc.

chose in possession, any asset that a person has in his possession with the exception of *choses-in-action.

C.I.F. *See* cost, insurance, and freight.

circular letter of credit, a letter from a banker to his agents or branches abroad authorizing the payment of a specific sum or sums of money to the holder of the letter.

circulating (working) capital, the available resources of a company estimated by deducting its *current liabilities from its *current assets.

City, short for the City of London, the centre of the U.K.'s financial activities, including banking, shipping, insurance, commodity markets, and the stock exchange.

civil engineer, an engineer qualified in the design, construction, and maintenance of large buildings, factories, roads, bridges, dams, canals, harbours, etc.

civil law, the law regulating private matters between citizens, as opposed to the *criminal law. It consists primarily of the law of *contract and the law of *tort.

civil servant, an employee in the public service working in a government department.

classified advertisement, a small advertisement in a newspaper placed according to class, e.g. jobs, houses, cars, etc.

clean bill of lading, a *bill of lading that contains no endorsements describing any defects in the goods or their packing when loaded for shipment. *Compare* dirty (foul) bill of lading.

clearing bank, a bank that is a member of the bankers *clearing house in London.

clearing house, an institution that arranges for the settlement of debts between its members. The best known is the bankers' clearing house, which settles debts each day between member banks. Commodity exchanges also often use a clearing house to settle debts between traders, brokers, etc.

clerk, a person employed in an office to keep records, make out invoices, arrange shipments, etc.

close company, a company defined by British law as one in which more than 50% of the share capital is controlled by five or fewer persons and their associates.

closed economy, a hypothetical country that neither imports nor exports and is, therefore, not affected by the economic policies of other countries.

closed indent, an order from abroad to an agent in the U.K. to purchase goods from a specified manufacturer. If the manufacturer is not specified the order would be described as an *open indent*.

closed shop, a place of employment in which membership of a trade union is a necessary requirement. *Compare* open shop.

close price, a share price in which there is only a small difference between the price at which a stockjobber is prepared to buy the shares and the price at which he is prepared to sell them.

closing date, 1. the final date upon which an application for a job, share issue, tender, etc., can be accepted. **2.** the date upon which a bid or offer expires.

closing prices, the prices at the end of a day's trading in a market, usually concerned with *commodities or with *shares on a *stock exchange.

coaster, a ship that plies along a coast, usually carrying locally produced goods, foodstuffs, etc.

coastguards, an organization originally concerned with the prevention of smuggling but now having wider duties as a coastal police force.

C.O.D. *See* cash on delivery.

code, 1. a series of numbers and letters forming part of an address. *See also* zip code. **2.** a series of numbers or letters used in telephone dialling to identify an area. **3.** *See* commercial codes.

collateral agreement, an agreement that is supplementary to a *contract or other agreement.

collateral security, something, such as a life-insurance policy or share certificate, given by a borrower to a lender as a security for a loan.

collecting banker, a banker who accepts cheques for the credit of a customer's account. The cheques are not cleared until they have been

collecting society

received and paid by the banker on whom they are drawn.

collecting society, a mutual-benefit insurance society, or friendly society, to which members make regular contributions to provide for ill-health, old-age, widowhood, etc.

collection charge, a charge made by a bank or other organization for collecting a debt.

collective bargaining, the process of negotiating conditions of work, pay, etc., between management and representatives of the employees, who are usually organized into a trade union.

collector of taxes, a person employed by a government department who is responsible for collecting the taxes assessed by an *inspector of taxes.

combination carrier, a ship that can carry combinations of bulk cargoes, such as oil and grain or oil and coal. *See also* bulk carrier.

combinations in restraint of trade, monopolistic agreements between companies to influence markets and prices to their advantage. Such practices are usually illegal.

commerce, trade or business in commodities or goods.

commercial bank. *See* joint-stock (commercial) bank.

commercial codes, codes used by companies to reduce the cost of sending telegrams or cables. Single code words represent whole sentences or phrases that are in common commercial use.

commercial traveller, a travelling agent who sells goods on behalf of his company. He may work for a salary, for commission, or for a combination of both.

commission, 1. payment made by a principal to a broker or agent, usually calculated on the basis of a percentage of the value of the goods bought or sold. **2.** payment made to a salesman by an employer and calculated on the basis of his sales. **3.** payment made to a bank or other commercial organization for changing money into a foreign currency, collecting a bill, etc.

commission agent, a person who buys or sells on behalf of a *principal and is paid in the form of a *commission.

committee, a group of people appointed or elected from a larger body to act or report on specific matters.

commodity, individual products, goods, or articles of trade, especially such raw materials as metals, fibres, sugar, cocoa, and rubber.

commodity broker, a *broker who deals on *commodity markets on behalf of users, importers, producers, and speculators.

commodity market, a market in which raw commodities, such as rubber, tin, jute, or sugar, are bought and sold. Trading is both for immediate delivery and in *futures. A *terminal market is one situated close to the users, but local markets often exist at principal ports of shipment. *Also called* commodity exchange.

Common Agricultural Policy (C.A.P.), the policy agreed by the member States of the European Economic Community (*see* Common Market) for fixing the prices of various agricultural products and, by various controls, to maintain these prices.

common carrier. *See* carrier.

Common Market (European Economic Community), a customs union and free trade area formed in 1957 by France, West Germany, Italy, the Netherlands, Belgium, and Luxembourg. It was later joined by Great Britain, Eire, and Denmark.

Common Stock, the U.S. name for *ordinary shares.

Commonwealth preference, a mutual arrangement between the U.K. and the commonwealth countries whereby certain goods can be imported at preferential rates of customs duties. Since the U.K. joined the Common Market it has been phased out.

company, an organization formed to enable a number of people to carry on a business. *See also* private company, public company, joint-stock company.

company law, detailed regulations as to the running of companies in the U.K. They are set out in the Companies Act of 1948 and 1967.

company seal, a seal embossed with the name of a company that must be imprinted on certain legal documents relating to the company.

company secretary, the employee of a company who is by law required to ensure that the company's affairs are carried out in accordance with the law.

competition, the state existing in an economy in which rivalry between producers or manufacturers of goods leads to lower prices.

competition and credit control, regulations by which the Bank of England controls monetary policy by establishing a *minimum lending rate, which controls the structure of interest rates generally.

compound interest, interest paid on the principal invested and on the interest earned (provided this is not paid out). The formula for calculating compound interest (I) is $I = P(1 + r/100)^n$, where P is the principal, r is the rate of interest, and n is the period.

comprehensive insurance, an insurance policy, usually taken out by motorists, which includes not only *third party risks but also covers damage to the insurer's car or loss through fire, theft, etc.

comptroller, a financial officer in charge of the accounts of an organization.

compulsory purchase, the power given to certain government departments to acquire property without necessarily having the consent of the owner. Compensation is payable. *Compare* requisitioning.

compulsory winding up, the closing-down of a business usually when the company concerned is *bankrupt or can no longer continue for some reason.

computer, an electronic calculating machine that can store and retrieve information (data) and reproduce it when required. Computers are widely used in commerce for keeping accounts, calculating payrolls, and stock control. *See* also analog computer; digital computer.

computer language, the code in which a *computer program is written. Several such codes are in use.

computer printout, the printed material produced by a *computer on demand, which sets out the information required.

computer program, a series of coded instructions that controls the operation of a computer. The programs are known as the *software*.

condition, a statement in a *contract that binds one party and allows the other party to repudiate the contract should the condition not be met.

conditional bill of sale, a *bill of sale in which the title to the goods referred to is not owned outright by the purchaser until certain conditions, such as the completion of payments on a *hire purchase agreement, have been fulfilled.

conditional order

conditional order, an order for goods given by a prospective purchaser, subject to stipulated conditions. Such an order may be conditional on the goods being delivered by a certain date or their quality reaching a specified standard.

conference lines, shipping lines that have agreed, in conference, to charge the same freight rates and passenger fares.

confidence trick, a swindle in which the victim's confidence is gained and he is then induced to part with money or property.

confirmed irrevocable letter of credit, a *confirmed letter of credit that cannot be cancelled by the purchaser before the expiry date, without the consent of the beneficiary.

confirmed letter of credit, a *letter of credit in which the seller's bank guarantees payment to the seller, or other named beneficiary, should the issuing bank fail to honour it.

confirming house, an agency that places orders with local exporters on behalf of overseas buyers. Such agencies guarantee payment and often finance the buyers.

conglomerate, an association of companies (usually subsidiary to a principal company) operating in various fields to reduce the risk of specialization.

consequential damages, the damage caused to a company by a disaster, such as a fire, which apart from material damage leads to a disruption of the business causing a loss of production.

consequential loss policy, an insurance policy to cover loss of profits, standing charges, etc., arising as a result of *consequential damages after a disaster.

consideration, the price paid by someone to enter into a *contract with another person.

consignee, the person to whom goods are sent as a result of a *contract of sale with another person (the *consignor).

consignment, a shipment or delivery of goods by a *consignor to a *consignee.

consignment note, a note accompanying a *consignment of goods. The document is made out by the *consignor, is handed to the *carrier, and is countersigned on delivery by the *consignee. Details of the goods and their insurances, etc., are included in the note.

consignor, a person who sends goods to another person (the *consignee) as a result of a *contract of sale.

consolidated accounts, the accounts of a group of companies that present the trading position of the group as a whole at the end of the financial year.

consolidated annuities (Consols), government *stock, not normally redeemable, that is issued from time to time at various rates of interest.

consolidated fund, the bank account, held by the Bank of England, into which taxes are paid and from which government expenditure is made.

Consols. See consolidated annuities.

consortium, an association of companies pooling their skills and resources to undertake a specific project. See also syndicate.

constructive total loss, a ship or a cargo that is not an *actual total loss may be so considered by the owners and abandoned because they are beyond economic repair. They are then declared a constructive total loss and the owners give notice of abandonment to the insurers, who then assume all rights to the property.

contra preferentum rule

consulage, the fee charged by a consul to certify an *invoice. *See* consular invoice.

consular invoice, a special invoice, legalized by a consul, that is sometimes required by the customs of an importing country to establish the *country of origin of imported goods. *See also* consulage.

consumer, a member of the public, regarded as a purchaser of manufactured goods, food, services, etc.

consumer advertising, publicizing the quality, merits, and price of goods or services directly to the final buyer.

consumer credit, any of several ways in which a member of the public can purchase goods on credit. They include *hire purchase, *credit cards, and credit accounts.

consumer durables, goods, such as refrigerators and washing machines, purchased by members of the public for use over a relatively long period.

consumer goods, goods, such as cars and TV sets, that are used by the public rather than in manufacturing other goods. *Compare* capital goods.

consumer nondurables (disposables), goods, such as food and drink, purchased by members of the public for immediate consumption.

consumer research, surveys amongst the general public to assess demand for a particular product or service.

consumption 1. (private consumption) expenditure by consumers on goods and services, such as food, drink, and entertainment. **2.** (public consumption) expenditure by government on education, health, etc.

containerization, a method of handling freight in which goods are packed in large rectangular containers. They are loaded onto ships in this form so that handling, risk of damage, and pilfering are kept to a minimum.

contemptuous damages, very small *damages awarded by a court in a civil action to indicate that in the court's view the case should never have been brought, although the person who brought it was technically in the right.

contingency insurance, an insurance policy that can cover many different types of risk, usually ones that are very unlikely to happen.

contingent annuity, an annuity that becomes payable if pre-defined circumstances arise. For example, a man may purchase an annuity for his wife, which is payable only if he dies before her. *Also called* reversionary annuity.

contingent liability, a debt that may arise as a result of some future event.

contract, a written or oral agreement between two or more persons that is legally enforceable.

contract by deed, a type of contract that is only legally enforceable if it is made by deed. In the U.K., for example, contracts transferring shares in statutory companies and *mortgages of land must be made of deed.

contract guarantee insurance, an insurance policy against the failure of a party to a *contract to play his part as agreed in the contract.

contract note, a document issued by a *stockbroker that gives legal evidence and details of a transaction to buy or sell shares.

contract of affreightment, a *contract made by a shipper with a shipowner for the carriage of cargo.

contra preferentum rule, if a written contract is ambiguous it is legally interpreted in the way that is least

25

control accounts

advantageous to the person who wrote the contract.

control accounts, double-entry bookkeeping accounts that give the totals of money received from debtors and money owing to creditors on a daily basis. These totals should agree with the sum of the monies received or paid out on that day by summarizing individual book accounts.

control chart, graphs used extensively in industry, usually for quality control, to indicate successive values of some variable factor. For example, the percentage of products turned out by a process that are defective would be plotted on a day-to-day basis.

conversion (in law), the unauthorized assumption and exercise of rights of ownership of property belonging to another.

conversion issue, a new issue of stock or shares to replace a security shortly due for redemption.

convertibility, the extent to which a currency can be freely exchanged for gold or for other currencies.

convertible debenture, a *debenture that is convertible into ordinary shares of the company on specified terms and usually on or after a specified date.

convertible term assurance, a *term insurance policy that is convertible to a *whole-life policy or to an *endowment policy without the necessity of the holder giving evidence as to his health. Such policies cost more than ordinary life policies.

copyright, the right, granted by law for a specified period, to an author to reproduce and distribute copies of literary, musical, or artistic works.

copy typist, a person trained to make typewritten copies of manuscripts, documents, etc. A copy typist is not expected to know shorthand or to take down letters. *Compare* shorthand typist, audio-typist.

corner, to buy such a large quantity of a commodity that the buyer is able to name his own price when selling it.

corporation, a group or association legally recognized as being a *chartered company, a *registered company, a *statutory company, or a local council.

corporation tax, the tax charged on a company's taxable profits.

cost accountant, an accountant trained to cost industrial processes in the interests of efficiency and economy.

cost and freight (C & F), contract terms in which the seller pays the cost of shipping the goods to their port of destination but the buyer is responsible for the cost of insuring them on the voyage.

cost-benefit analysis, an evaluation of a projected investment that unlike an ordinary commercial investment appraisal, takes into account various environmental and social factors affecting the desirablity or otherwise of the proposal.

cost-centre (in accountancy), the part of a business organization to which costs can legitimately be attributed. The object of identifying cost centres is to analyse the areas in a business that produce costs so that their affect on profits can be examined.

cost effectiveness, an analysis of the costs incurred in running a business to check that the company is obtaining the optimum output for its expenditure.

cost, insurance, and freight (C.I.F.), contract terms in which the seller pays the cost of shipping the goods

credit

to their port of destination and for insuring them on the voyage.

cost-of-living bonus, an allowance given to employees of a company because the cost of living has risen; the rise may be temporary and some companies wish to avoid raising salaries, which cannot easily be reduced and may also involve increases in pensions.

cost-of-living index, an index providing a periodic review of the changes in the prices of goods and services, which indicates the average cost of living. *Also called* retail price index.

cost-plus contract, a type of contract in which goods or services are sold on the basis of their cost, plus an agreed percentage to cover the overheads and profit of the supplier.

cost unit, any part of a manufactured article or a service that, from an accountancy point of view, has an identifiable cost.

counterbid, the reply of a buyer to a *counter offer made by a seller. If the seller's counter offer is unacceptable to the buyer he may make a counterbid on terms that he hopes the seller will accept.

counterclaim, the reply to a claim for damages in which a person tries to offset part or all of the damages claimed against him or to set out his own claim for damages.

counteroffer, the reply of a seller to a *bid made by a buyer. If a firm makes an offer to sell goods at a certain price on certain terms a buyer may make a bid at a lower price or on more advantageous terms. If the seller finds the bid unacceptable he may make a counteroffer, which is usually at a price or on terms intermediate between the original offer and the bid. The buyer may accept the counteroffer or make a *counterbid.

countervailing credit, a *letter of credit given by a U.K. agency, such as a merchant bank, to a foreign buyer in cases in which the seller wishes to conceal his identity. The agency substitutes documents made out in their own name for documents made out in the seller's name. *Also called* back-to-back credit.

countervailing duty, an *import duty levied by a country to counteract unfair competitive practices by other countries, i.e. to prevent the prices of imported goods from undercutting domestically produced goods.

country of origin, the country from which a shipment of commodities originates.

coupon, a separable part of a certificate, usually a *bearer bond, that when detached from the bond can be presented by the holder of the bond to obtain payment of the interest or dividend due.

cover, 1. the number of times by which the net profit of a company available for distribution exceeds the amount of dividends actually distributed to the shareholders. **2.** an insurance policy that provides for a specific risk.

cover note, a temporary document issued by an insurance company to indicate that a risk is covered, pending the issue of the policy.

craft union, a *trade union comprising all the workers in a country that have the same skills. They may work in different industries. *See also* industrial union, general union.

crawling peg, a form of *exchange-rate control in which the rate of exchange of a country's currency is allowed to move in response to supply and demand, but only by limited amounts each month. *Also called* sliding peg.

credit, 1. the ability to obtain goods

credit card

without paying for them immediately. **2.** a favourable balance on an account. **3.** the right-hand page of an account book showing money received. **4.** *short for* letter of credit.

credit card, an identification card issued by a bank or department store enabling the holder to obtain goods on *credit.

credit insurance, an insurance against loss resulting from granting credit to a firm that fails to pay for whatever reason.

credit note, a note issued by a trader showing the amount of money owing to a customer usually as the result of the return of goods (unwanted or defective) or an error in an account.

creditor, a person to whom money is owed. *Compare* debtor.

creditors' voluntary liquidation, the winding-up of a company when the *liquidator is not satisfied that the directors volunteering to wind-up the company are able to comply with their declaration that their company will be able to meet their debts in full within twelve months.

credit rating, the standing of a person (or firm) in relation to his ability to repay any loans made to him.

credit squeeze, a restriction imposed by governments to limit the amount of *credit extended by banks, etc., so that hire purchase becomes more difficult and more expensive. The intention is to reduce the activity of an economy.

credit transfer, a means of transferring funds through a bank in settlement of debts. *Also called* bank giro.

crossed cheque, a *cheque drawn on a bank marked with two parallel lines (in ink or printed) indicating that the cheque is not freely negotiable for cash on demand but that it must be paid into a bank account.

cubic capacity, the volume of a space (such as a cargo hold or engine cylinder) expressed in cubic metres or cubic centimetres or in cubic yards or cubic feet.

cum dividend, denoting a share price when the purchaser is entitled to receive the next dividend. *Compare* ex dividend.

cum new, denoting a share price when the *shares offered for sale include the right to any *scrip issue or *rights issue.

currency, 1. the money in circulation in a country whether in coin or in paper. **2.** *See* currency of a bill.

currency of a bill, the time between the drawing of a *bill of exchange and the date on which it becomes payable.

current account, an account kept at a bank by a customer for day-to-day transactions. *Compare* deposit account, budget account.

current assets, the assets of a company, e.g. stock, finished products, cash in hand, etc., that are used to finance the costs of generating further income.

current liabilities, the sums of money that a company has to pay out within a financial year. These include payments due to trade creditors for materials or services supplied, declared dividends, and taxation liabilities. *Compare* deferred liabilities.

current yield (flat yield), the *yield on a *fixed-interest security calculated as the percentage of the purchase price represented by the gross annual yield. It does not take into account any loss or gain on redemption.

curriculum vitae, Latin for the course of a person's life. An account of a person's career and qualifications, usually for the purpose of employment.

custom of trade, in the settlement of disputes arising from trade contracts it is, in some cases, acceptable to assume that certain terms are implied by the contract if they are the custom of the trade concerned.

Customs and Excise, a tax-collecting department of the U.K. government, originally concerned with the collection of *excise duties and the prevention of smuggling. It is now concerned with the administration and collection of a wide range of *indirect taxes, including duties on tobacco and drink, *V.A.T., etc., in addition to customs duties.

customs assigned number, a registered exporter may be assigned a number by the Customs and Excise department permitting him to export goods without going through the normal procedures (e.g. *pre-entry procedure). This number must be quoted on the *bill of lading.

customs clearance, the procedure for obtaining the consent of the Customs and Excise department for the import or export of dutiable goods.

custom's tariff, a list of goods showing those upon which import duty is payable. It is published in the Customs of a country.

customs union, an agreement between countries that there should be no customs duties payable on goods exported from one to the other. A common rate of import duties is often fixed for countries that are not members of the union.

cut-throat competition, a very competitive market in which traders are prepared to operate at very low margins of profit in order to eliminate competitors.

cwt. *See* hundredweight.

D

damages, an award made by a court of law to a party in a civil action as monetary compensation for loss or injury sustained.

danger money, the payment of higher wages to a person performing a hazardous job.

data processing, the collection and arrangement of data and other information by the use of *computers so that the information can be retrieved in any desired way.

dated securites, securities that are repayable during a specified period in the future. They are broadly classified as being repayable within five years (short-dated stocks); repayable between five and fifteen years (medium-dated stocks); and repayable after fifteen years (long-dated stocks).

date of maturity, the date on which a *bill of exchange, a security, an insurance policy, etc., is due to be exchanged for cash.

date stamp, a device for stamping dates on documents or mail.

day books, books of account in which all transactions carried out in a business are entered on a daily basis.

days of grace, the number of days allowed, usually as a gesture of goodwill, between the due date of a *bill of exchange, insurance premium, etc., and the date on which action would be taken to recover the funds, the policy allowed to lapse, etc.

deadweight tonnage, the weight of a ship in long tons, including crew, stores, fresh water, cargo, etc., when loaded to the *load line.

dear money, money that can only be borrowed at a high rate of interest. *Compare* cheap money.

death certificate, an official certificate signed by a medical practitioner to certify the date and cause of death.

death duties, tax paid on the inheritance of money or property. *See also* capital transfer tax, estate duty.

death rate, the number of deaths per 1000 of the population in a particular year.

debenture, a certificate or bond issued by a company acknowledging a loan and stating the terms of repayment and the fixed rate of interest that will be paid.

debit, 1. an entry of a sum in an account book. 2. the left-hand page of an account book showing money owed.

debit note, a note sent to a customer informing him that his account has been, or will be, *debited, often because the customer has been undercharged for goods supplied.

debt, money or some other asset owed by one person or company to another.

debt collector, a person employed to collect debts on behalf of a *creditor.

debtor, a person who owes money to another. *Compare* creditor.

decimal currency, a currency based on the decimal system. Usually the standard unit is divided into 100 sub-units.

decimal notation, a number system using the base 10. The metric system of units is based on the decimal notation.

deck cargo, cargo carried on the open deck of a ship rather than in its hold.

declared value, the value of a company's stock declared for tax purposes.

decreasing term assurance, a form of life assurance policy issued for a specified period and payable only if the assured dies within that period. If the period specified is of considerable length, for example in connection with a *mortgage, the sum assured in the event of death decreases each year as the loan is repaid. *See also* term assurance.

deductible, 1. denoting the part of a claim against an insurance policy that the policyholder agrees to pay. *See also* excess policy. **2.** Denoting a payment that is allowable as a business expense and may be deducted from income for tax purposes.

deductions at source, an economical method of collecting income tax due in which an organization deducts the tax from the individual before paying him his salary, dividends, etc., and passes the tax collected on to the tax authorities.

deed, a document containing an agreement or contract that is enforceable by law. It is signed, sealed, and delivered by one party to the other. *See also* contract by deed.

deed of arrangement, a *deed that enables a debtor to avoid *bankruptcy by agreeing to pay off his creditors in part or in whole. *See also* deed of assignment, deed of inspectorship.

deed of assignment, a *deed of arrangement in which a debtor assigns all of his property to a trustee for the benefit of his creditors.

deed of covenant, a *deed in which a person contracts to pay a fixed sum to someone or to a charity for a fixed period, usually seven years. Such a deed often enables a saving in tax to be made.

deed of inspectorship, a *deed of arrangement in which a debtor hands over his business to the charge of an inspector appointed by his creditors.

deferred annuity, an *annuity that is paid some years after the premium or premiums have been received.

deferred assets, *assets that are neither fixed nor current.

deferred liabilities, sums of money that a company does not have to pay out within a financial year. *Compare* current liabilities.

deferred payment, a payment that is held back until some date in the future, usually by agreement.

deferred rate, a *rebate made at regular intervals by shipping companies to their customers provided the company obtains the exclusive right to ship the customers' goods to particular destinations.

deferred taxation, tax that will become due for payment by a company but that has been deferred by the tax authorities.

deficit, the amount by which a sum of money is too small, especially the amount by which a government's revenue is less than the money it spends.

deflation, a general reduction in prices owing to a decrease in the economic activity of a nation affecting national income, industrial output, and employment. *See also* disinflation.

defunct company, a *limited liability company that has been *wound-up and no longer operates.

delcredere agent, an agent who obtains orders for goods from a buyer and also guarantees that the buyer will pay for them.

delegate

delegate, a person sent to a conference, etc., to represent an organization.

delegation, 1. the act or process of entrusting authority, work, etc., to a deputy. **2.** a number of delegates forming a deputation or body of representatives.

delivered docks, contract terms in which the seller pays for delivering goods for export to the shipping docks to await shipment to the port of destination. He does not pay for loading them on to the ship. *Compare* free on board.

delivery, a consignment of goods in total or part fulfilment of a *contract.

delivery date, the date stipulated in a *contract upon which a seller has agreed to deliver goods to a buyer.

delivery free, contract terms in which the seller agrees to pay all delivery charges.

delivery note, a formal note, usually in duplicate, accompanying goods delivered to a buyer who keeps one copy and endorses the other as evidence of delivery.

demarcation dispute, a dispute between trades unions or members of trades unions regarding the division between types of work carried out.

demography, the study of human populations, birth rates, death rates, etc.

demurrage, a penalty that is paid to a ship-owner if his ship is delayed in a port by failure to load or unload the cargo on time.

department store, a large retail shop with several departments, each selling a different type of goods.

deposit, an amount of money paid by a *buyer either to reserve goods or property that he wishes to buy at a later date or as the first of a series of instalments.

deposit account, a bank account in which money is deposited to earn interest. *Compare* current account.

depositary, a person with whom something is deposited, especially one who acts as a trustee.

depositor, one who deposits money in a bank.

depository, a storeplace or warehouse.

depreciation, a decrease in the value of an asset, such as a car or a piece of machinery, as a result of continued use or of becoming out-of-date.

depression, an economic situation in which demand for goods falls so that industry has to reduce its output, causing unemployment and a reduction in investment. This is the low point of the *trade cycle.

despatch note, a note from a seller to a buyer informing him that the goods he has ordered have been despatched.

destination, the place to which a seller agrees to deliver goods, and to pay shipping and delivery charges, in fulfilment of a contract.

devaluation, a reduction in the value of a country's currency in terms of gold or of another country's currency.

developing countries, countries, such as those in Asia, Africa, and Latin America, that have large populations, low standards of living, and a largely agricultural economy.

development areas, regions of high unemployment. In the U.K. the government provides incentives of various kinds to encourage the growth of industry in these areas.

dictating machine, a machine that records speech so that it can then be replayed either for record purposes or for transcription by a typist.

discount house

dies non (Latin. Short for *dies non juridicus*), a day upon which no legal business can be done.

different account, an account used when goods, shares, etc., have been sold by one party to another and then bought back before the buyer has paid for them. The account shows only the difference between the sale and purchase values as owing.

digital computer, a type of computer in which data is stored and operated on in the form of digits; numbers and letters being coded in the form of the binary digits 0 and 1. *Compare* analog computer.

dilapidations, 1. repairs that are necessary to premises at the end of a tenancy. **2.** the cost of carrying out these repairs.

diploma, an official document setting out the holder's qualifications in a particular subject or skill.

direct debits, an arrangement made by a purchaser with his bank enabling the seller to have his bank account credited and the purchaser's account debited with the cost of goods or services supplied.

direct labour, the workers in an industry who are directly concerned with manufacturing processes. *Compare* indirect labour.

direct-mail shot, sales literature sent through the post direct to potential customers.

directors, persons appointed to manage a company on behalf of the shareholders.

directors' fees, special payments made to *directors. The payments are usually nominal.

directory, an alphabetical list of the names and addresses of the people in a particular area, trade, etc.

direct selling, the sale of goods by a manufacturer directly to a consumer, omitting the *wholesaler and the *retailer.

direct taxation, income tax and other taxes paid directly by individuals or companies to the taxation authorities. *Compare* indirect taxation.

dirty (foul) bill of lading, a *bill of lading endorsed by the captain or mate of the ship in which goods are to be transported, certifying that the goods were defective or damaged when they arrived at the docks for loading on to the ship. *Compare* clean bill of lading.

dirty float, an exchange-rate policy in which a country's currency is nominally allowed to be free of restriction but is subject to occasional discreet intervention by the country's government to influence movements in the rates. *See also* free (floating) exchange rates.

discharged bankrupt, a debtor who has been made *bankrupt and who has successfully applied to a court for the grant of an absolute or conditional discharge from the bankruptcy.

disclaimer, a statement in which a person or company denies responsibility for a particular occurrence.

discount, 1. a reduction in the price of a commodity for payment in cash, for prompt payment, or for bulk purchases. **2.** to purchase a *bill of exchange for less than its face value before its maturity date.

discount broker, a broker who arranges the purchases and sales of *bills of exchange on a commission basis.

discounted bill, a *bill of exchange purchased by a third party at a *discount because the bill has not yet matured.

discount house, a bank that deals in the discounting of *bills of exchange, treasury bills, etc.

discount market

discount market, a market that deals with *bills of exchange, *treasury bills, *trade bills, *bank bills, etc.

discount rate, the rate at which a *bill of exchange can be discounted.

discretionary trust, a *trust in which the trustees have discretion to select the beneficiaries from a class of nominated persons.

discriminating tariff, an *import duty that is not the same for all the countries with which a nation has trade agreements. Goods from some countries may be liable to a high import duty, whereas the same goods coming from another country may pay less duty or even no duty at all.

dishonour, to refuse to honour a *bill, *draft, or *cheque by making the necessary payment.

disinflationary policy, measures introduced by a government to check inflation. It usually involves maintaining the purchasing power of its currency by limiting credit or raising interest rates.

displacement tonnage, the weight of a ship in long tons, including all its machinery but excluding ballast.

display unit, a cabinet, counter, stand, etc., used in a shop to display goods offered for sale.

disposable income, the income remaining to a person after he has paid *direct taxes.

disposables. See consumer nondurables.

distillery, a factory in which alcoholic spirits are manufactured.

distressed area, an area of a country in which there is high unemployment.

distressed goods, goods that are faulty or damaged in some way and are offered for sale at a very low price.

distributable reserves, the reserves of a company from which payments, such as dividends, are made to shareholders.

distribution, a payment made by a company from profits or from *distributable reserves, usually to its shareholders.

diversification, expansion by a company into an industry outside its normal field of activity. For example, a company that usually manufactures bicycles may decide to diversify into washing machines.

dividend, the proportion of the profits of a company that is distributed to its shareholders at the end of the company's financial year. See also interim dividend.

dividend cover, the number of times the *distributable profits of a company exceeds the actual distribution made to ordinary shareholders as dividends. If the former exceeds the latter by a factor of five, then the dividends would be said to be covered five times.

dividend limitation, a government order to companies requiring them to limit increases in dividends in the interests of curbing *inflation.

dividend warrant, a notification in the form of a cheque issued by a company to a shareholder in payment of a *dividend. The warrant usually includes details of the shareholding, the rate of the dividend, and information as to whether tax has been deducted or not.

division of labour, the principle of organizing work, particularly in a factory, where each worker is responsible for carrying out a specific task in the process of producing goods. It is the essential requirement upon which *mass production is based.

dock dues, a tax or toll levied on all ships entering or leaving a port.

docker, a labourer employed at a port for loading or unloading ship's cargoes.

dock receipt, a receipt acknowledging that goods have been delivered to a dock for shipment.

dock warrant, a document of *title proving the ownership of goods stored in a warehouse at a dock.

dockyard, a place in which ships are built, repaired, or fitted out.

documentary bill, a *bill of exchange together with such other documents as the insurance policy, invoice, and *bill of lading of the related goods.

documentary credit. *See* letter of credit.

documents against acceptance (D/A), payment terms for exported goods in which the shipping documents, together with a draft for the sum due, are sent by the seller to a bank or agent at the port of destination. The bank gives the buyer the shipping documents on acceptance of the draft.

documents against presentation (D/P). *See* cash against documents.

dollar premium, the price that a U.K. resident has to pay to convert sterling into U.S. dollars for the purpose of purchasing U.S. or Canadian securities.

donee, a person who is given something by a *donor.

donor, a person who gives property or money by gift or legacy to another or to a charity.

door-to-door selling, a form of *direct selling in which the representatives of a manufacturer tour round a district knocking on doors and attempting to sell their wares to housewives, etc., on the doorstep.

double-entry book-keeping, an accounting procedure enabling a company's books to be balanced. The principle is that every *debit entry has a *credit entry so that at any time the total debit balances should equal the total credit balances.

double option, an *option that entitles its buyer either to buy or to sell shares, commodities, etc., at their current price within a specified period. It is a combination of a *call option and a *put option and as it is expensive to buy a marked movement in price must be anticipated to make it worthwhile.

double pricing, a method of pricing goods for sale in which cards attached to them indicate two prices, the higher of which is deleted to indicate the extent of the bargain being offered.

double taxation, income derived from overseas that is taxed in the country of origin and is again taxed when remitted to the home country of the person or company that has earned the income. Many countries by reciprocal agreements will grant double-taxation relief in such cases.

doubtful debt, a debt that may not be recoverable. Reserves may be set aside out of a company's profits to meet this eventuality.

down payment, 1. an initial deposit made on a purchase to demonstrate the serious intent of the purchaser and to reserve the goods in question. **2.** the initial payment made by a purchaser buying something on *hire purchase.

draft, a written order to a bank to pay a specified sum of money to the person named in the draft.

draft agreement, a preliminary agreement subject to further revision by the parties concerned.

draught, the depth of water needed by a ship in order to float.

draughtsman, a person trained to

drawback

make engineering drawings, architectural plans, etc.

drawback, repayment of customs duties paid when materials imported are subsequently re-exported or used to manufacture goods that are exported.

drawee, 1. the person to whom a *bill of exchange is addressed. He is responsible for paying it on maturity. **2.** the banker on whom a cheque is drawn.

drawer, 1. the person who draws up a *bill of exchange ordering the *drawee to pay the stated amount. **2.** the person who signs a cheque ordering a bank to pay the amount stated to the person mentioned.

dry dock, a structure that when filled with water can accommodate a ship for repairs: once in the dock the water is pumped out making the hull of the ship accessible.

due date, the date upon which a *bill of exchange is payable.

dumping, the export of surplus goods at a low profit, or even at a loss, in order to maintain prices in the home market.

durables. *See* consumer durables.

duress, the use of coercion to influence someone to sign a contract or to render a contract void.

dutiable, subject to the payment of import duties.

duty, a tax imposed on the import, export, sale, or manufacture of goods, property, etc.

E

E. & O.E. *See* errors and omissions excepted.

earned income, income earned as a result of paid employment or of self-employment. For tax purposes, in some countries, earned income attracts less tax than *unearned income.

earnings, wages, salaries, or profits.

earnings per share, the *available earnings of a company, divided by the number of ordinary shares.

earnings yield, the *yield that a share would produce if all the *available earnings of the company were distributed in dividends.

easement, a right entitling a person to make use of the land of another person, for example, as a right of way.

easy money. *Another name for* cheap money.

economic cost, the total cost of an enterprise taking into account that some of the factors of production could possibly have been utilized in a more profitable way. *Compare* accounting cost.

economic growth, the expansion of a national economy resulting from the interplay of the following factors: growth in the population (providing more labour), growth in investment, and growth in technological improvements.

economics, the study of the production, distribution, and consumption of goods and services and their effects on the welfare of mankind.

economic sanctions, the economic measures taken by a country or a group of countries to bring pressure on another country in order to change its policies. Sanctions can include *embargoes on trade and restrictions on capital investment in the country concerned.

economies of scale, a reduction in the average cost of production of a product or industry as output rises.

EDP. *See* electronic data processing.

education endowment, an endowment assurance, usually on the life of a parent to provide regular sums of money to pay for a child's school or university fees.

E.E.C. *See* Common Market.

EFTA. *See* European Free Trade Association.

electronic data processing, the use of computers for manipulating information, especially business information.

embargo, 1. an order prohibiting the import or export of certain goods, usually for political reasons. **2.** an order forbidding ships to enter or leave a port, usually before the outbreak of a war. **3.** a decision by a trade union not to unload a ship or use goods from a country with which it is not in sympathy.

embezzlement, the fraudulent use by an employee of his employer's money or property.

emolument, wages, salary, fees, etc., arising from office or from employment.

employee, a person who is paid for working for another person or a company.

employer, a person who employs others and pays them for their work.

employers' liability insurance

employers' liability insurance, an insurance policy that gives an employer cover against liability to employees for incurring injury or disease in the course of their employment.

employment agencies, agencies that bring employers into contact with prospective employees.

endorsement, a signature on the back of a *bill of exchange or a cheque, indicating that the original payee agrees that it may be transferred.

endow, to provide an institution with a source of income as a gift.

endowment assurance, a life insurance policy in which the sum assured (together with profits earned) is payable to the holder at the end of a specified period or to his estate on his death.

enquiry. *See* inquiry.

entrepôt trade, a form of trade in which goods are shipped from their port of origin to some large international port, such as London or Rotterdam, and are later re-exported to some other port.

entrepreneur, a person who organizes and backs an enterprise with capital in order to make profits.

equity, 1. legal rules and practice to give redress to a person that cannot otherwise be obtained under common or statute law. **2.** the interest of a shareholder of common stock in a company. **3.** stocks and shares not bearing fixed interest.

equity-linked policies, insurance policies in which the insurers invest their premium income in a wide range of *equities.

ergonomics, the study of work and how it is carried out by workers in industry, with the object of improving performance and output.

errors and omissions excepted (E. & O.E.), the words or initials often added to an invoice or to a bank statement to absolve the issuer from the consequences of clerical errors.

escalation clause, a clause, in a *contract permitting an increase in the agreed price should costs rise above an agreed limit.

escape clause, a clause in a contract that permits one of the parties, in certain circumstances, to avoid penalties for failure to fulfil his obligations.

escrow, a deed or contract held by a third person that does not come into effect until certain conditions have been fulfilled.

estate, 1. property or possessions. **2.** the property and interests of a deceased person.

estate agent, 1. a person or company that acts as an intermediary between the buyer and the seller of land, properties, houses, etc. **2.** a valuer and auctioneer of *real estate and leasehold property.

estate duty, death duty. This is now superseded in the U.K. by *capital transfer tax.

estimate, a formal statement of the cost of carrying out a certain piece of work. For example, builders give estimates for repairing houses, etc.

estimator, someone who works out the estimates prepared by a company.

estoppel, a legal term used when a person is prevented from denying a statement he has made orally or in writing and upon which some other person has acted in good faith.

eurodollars, U.S. dollars held by banks in Europe and used to finance international trade. They stand at a premium over normal dollars as they are not subject to U.S. trade regulations.

European Economic Community (E.E.C.). *See* Common Market.

European Free Trade Association (EFTA), a trade association formed in 1959 between Austria, Denmark, Norway, Portugal, Sweden, Switzerland, and the U.K. After the U.K. and Denmark joined the *Common Market EFTA was greatly weakened.

eviction, the expulsion of a tenant from land or property by legal process.

ex, 1. without, excluding, e.g. *ex dividend. 2. out of, sold from, e.g. *ex warehouse. 3. former, e.g. ex-director.

excess capacity, spare resources of manpower and machinery that enable a company to increase its production without increasing its *average cost.

excess demand, a market situation in which the demand for a product exceeds the supply.

excess policy, an insurance policy containing the condition that where damage occurs (to a motor-car or to property, etc.) the policy holder will be responsible for a specified sum in regard to each claim, the balance being paid by the insurance company.

excess supply, a market situation in which the supply of a product exceeds the demand for it.

exchange control, measures introduced by the government of a country to restrict the outflow of capital. They include restrictions on the export of currency for investment abroad and approval to purchase foreign currency.

exchange rate, the price of a currency in a foreign exchange market.

exchange restriction, a measure of *exchange control to limit the purchase of foreign currency and the sale of domestic currency.

excise duty, tax imposed on goods produced within a country. Some countries impose an excise duty on alcoholic drinks and tobacco.

exclusive agent. *See* agent.

ex dividend, denoting a share price when the purchaser is not entitled to the next dividend due. This is because the dividend is payable within a month and the price of the share has been adjusted accordingly.

executive, 1. a person having administrative authority within a company or organization. 2. *short for* executive committee. The body that runs an organization, such as a trade union.

executor, a person who administers the estate of a testator in accordance with his will.

exemplary damages, damages granted in a court action that reflect the court's wish to punish the unsuccessful party as well as to compensate the successful party.

ex gratia, describing a gift or payment made, without legal obligation, as an act of grace.

expected inflation, an anticipated general rise in prices that is anticipated so generally that it is reflected in all contracts entered into.

expense account, an account of expenditure incurred by an *employee in the course of his official duties. This expenditure will usually either be refunded by his company or deductible for tax purposes.

expert's report, a report made by a person who has a special knowledge or skill in some field. Such a report is often required in the case of an insurance claim, arbitration, or legal case.

expiry, the termination of an agreement, licence, passport, etc.

export, to sell goods manufactured in

export house

one's own country to customers in a foreign country.

export house, an agency possessing the experience necessary to assist manufacturers in selling their goods abroad. They sell on commission and may help manufacturers by paying on delivery of the goods or by guaranteeing payment.

export-import bank, a bank established by the U.S. Government to encourage international trade with America by making loans.

export incentive, tax relief, subsidies, bonus, or credit granted by governments to companies to encourage increased exports.

export leasing, a method of exporting goods, such as machinery, in which the machinery or equipment is purchased by a leasing company, usually in its country of manufacture, and is then leased to an overseas buyer. This arrangement enables the buyer to use the machinery even if he cannot obtain funds or permission to purchase it, and the manufacturer to be paid in full.

export packing, a specially strong form of packing for goods that will withstand transit by sea or air.

exports, goods and services sold to foreign countries.

ex quay, contract terms for the sale of goods in which the seller pays the delivery charges to the port of destination and for loading the goods on to rail or road transport at the quay. Thereafter, the buyer is responsible for transport charges.

ex ship, contract terms in which the seller pays for all shipping charges to the port of destination and for the cost of unloading the goods from the ship. He does not, however, pay for lighter charges or dock charges.

extraordinary general meeting, a meeting of a company called by the *directors or by the shareholders (usually holding not less than 10% of the voting shares). *Compare* annual general meeting.

ex warehouse, contract terms in which the buyer pays for all the charges of delivery, except for the cost of loading the goods from the seller's warehouse on to the road or rail transport.

ex works, contract terms in which the price includes the cost of loading the goods on to road or rail transport but the buyer is responsible for all other delivery charges.

F

face value, the value stated on an object or document as opposed to its market value, especially the *par value of a security.

factor, 1. a trader who buys goods in bulk and sells them on a wholesale basis. **2.** a company that buys the debts of other businesses and collects them on its own behalf, thus providing working capital for the businesses concerned (invoice discounting). This function may be combined with *credit insurance.

factoring, the business of a *factor, especially the purchasing and servicing of debts.

factory cost, the cost of manufacturing a product. It is the factory cost that after mark-up for profit becomes the selling price.

fair average quality (f.a.q.), a quality description for goods (especially natural commodities) that are sold neither on sample nor on specification but on the understanding that their quality will be equal to the average of recent deliveries or the average for the current crop.

falling market, a market in which prices have fallen and are expected to fall further.

family allowance, money paid to parents of families by the government as a social-service benefit.

f.a.q. See fair average quality.

f.a.s. See free alongside ship.

fate, the payment or non-payment of a cheque. See also advise fate.

feasibility study, a detailed investigation of an idea or project to attempt to discover whether or not it will be both technically possible and commercially successful.

feeding stuffs, substances, either in their original form or compounded into pellets, cake, etc., that are fed to farm animals. Compare foodstuffs.

fiat money, money that has the backing of the state to be treated as legal tender, although it is not backed by reserves. Paper money is an example. See also fiduciary issue.

fictitious asset, an entry, such as a trading loss, that appears in the asset column of a company's accounts for book-keeping reasons, although it has no realizable asset value.

fidelity guarantee insurance, a form of insurance in which an employer takes out a policy to protect himself against the possibility of dishonesty amongst his employees.

fiduciary issue, an issue of bank notes that is backed by government securities rather than gold.

field study, a planned study of the market for a product based on personal interviews with potential users.

FIFO. See first in, first out.

file, 1. a collection of letters or documents arranged within a folder. **2.** a block of data stored in a computer memory.

filing cabinet, a piece of office furniture consisting of several large drawers in which *files are stored.

final dividend, the last distribution of profits in the form of a *dividend to shareholders made by a company in

41

final invoice

a particular year. *Compare* interim dividend.

final invoice, an invoice giving the full details of a consignment of goods, including exact delivered weights, etc. It follows a *proforma invoice, which is often sent before the full details are known.

finance company, a company that specializes in the financing of *hire-purchase agreements.

Financial Times Industrial Ordinary Share Index, a UK share index indicating general movements of share prices since 1935. It is based on 30 representative UK companies.

financial year, a period of 12 months in respect of which a company's *accounts are made up. It can start on any date but often begins on January 1st or April 6th.

financier, a person who provides money to help other people run their businesses.

fine, a sum of money that must be paid as a penalty for having committed an offence against the law.

fineness, a measure of the purity of precious metals, especially gold and silver. It is the number of parts of the pure metal in 1000 parts of the impure substance.

fine trade bill, a *trade bill having the backing of a first-class bank or finance company.

fine tuning, economic measures, such as changes in the money supply, taxation, or public expenditure, designed to control *inflation or *balance of payment problems on a short-term basis.

fire insurance, the form of insurance that offers protection against loss or damage resulting from fire.

firm, 1. a business or professional organization based on a *partnership. 2. any business organization.

firm market, a market in which there are more buyers than sellers and in which, consequently, prices remain steady or have an upward tendency.

firm offer, an offer to sell goods or services on stated terms that remains in force for a stated time. Before the offer expires the person to whom it was made can accept it or not, but if he makes a *counteroffer the offer is no longer in force.

first in, first out (FIFO), a method of valuing the stock of raw materials of a business, based on the assumption that the stock to be used first was the stock that was delivered first (i.e. that has been on the premises for the longest time). This method makes the remaining stock dear in times of inflation. *Compare* last in, first out.

first-loss policy, a type of insurance policy in which the sum assured is less than the total value of the goods at risk, but both parties agree that the rules of *average do not apply.

first of exchange, the top copy of a *bill of exchange.

fiscal policy, the policy of a government in relation to taxation and public spending.

fiscal year, the 12-month period that constitutes the year of account of a government.

fixed assets, capital equipment, such as machinery, purchased by a company and shown in its *accounts. *See also* depreciation.

fixed costs. *See* indirect costs.

fixed exchange rate, a currency *exchange rate that a government attempts to keep at a fixed level by increasing or decreasing its reserves. *Compare* floating exchange rate.

fixed-interest security, a security that yields interest at a fixed and stated rate. Debentures, government

foreclose

bonds, and preference shares all fall into this class.

flag discrimination, reluctance by a nation to permit its goods to be carried by ships of other nations.

flag of convenience, a flag flown by a ship indicating that it belongs to a certain nation, such as Panama or Liberia, when it actually originates elsewhere. Registrations of this kind are used to reduce taxation and the cost of carrying out strict crew regulations.

flat, a type of barge with a flat bottom, used to transport goods in shallow waters.

flat rate, a charge or payment that does not change, irrespective of the number of items, people, visits, etc. For example, a doctor may be paid at a flat rate for attending a clinic, irrespective or the number of patients he sees.

flat yield. *See* current yield.

fleet rating, a special price given to the owner of a number of vehicles, for insurance, repairs, etc., provided that the service is provided for all that owner's vehicles.

flexible trust, a form of *unit trust in which the investments can be changed at any time by the managers.

floating charge, a security over all the assets of a company that has borrowed money, rather than over specific assets. *Compare* specific charge.

floating debenture, a *debenture secured by a *floating charge.

floating exchange rate, a currency *exchange rate that a government permits to fluctuate with supply and demand. *Compare* fixed exchange rate. *See also* sliding.

floating policy, an insurance policy in which the type of risk is specified but not the value of the goods. In marine insurance, a floating policy may be used to cover all the goods shipped by a company in a year. At the end of the year the premium will be adjusted according to the total quantity shipped.

floating warranty, a guarantee given by one person to another that induces this person to enter into a contract with a third person.

floor trader, a member of a market, such as a commodity exchange, stock exchange, etc., who is permitted to trade on the floor of the market.

flotation, the process of raising funds for a company by selling shares in it or by borrowing money from a bank.

flotsam and jetsam, the wreckage of a ship and its cargo floating upon the sea or cast ashore.

flow chart, a diagram showing how products flow through a production line, how chemicals flow through a process, etc.

fluctuating market, a market in which prices rise and fall unpredictably.

fluctuating rate, an exchange rate that varies unpredictably from day to day.

F.O.B. *See* free on board.

foodstuffs, basic foods for human consumption. *Compare* feeding stuffs.

F.O.Q. *See* free on quay.

F.O.R. *See* free on rail.

forced loan, a loan made because the borrower has no option but to borrow (because he needs the money) or because the lender has no option but to lend (because he is ordered to do so by a government, etc.).

forecasting, predicting the future trends of a market, either in the short-term or the long-term.

foreclose, to sell the property of someone who has mortgaged an

foreign currency allowance

asset as a security against a loan and who cannot make an agreed repayment or an interest payment.

foreign currency allowance, a permitted amount of a foreign currency that a resident of a country is allowed to buy, especially if the foreign currency is required for travelling.

foreign exchange, 1. the changing of the currency of one nation into that of another nation. **2.** the foreign currency.

foreign exchange broker, a dealer who specializes in buying and selling foreign currencies, for a *brokerage.

foreign exchange market, the market that deals in foreign currencies. Rates of exchange fluctuate from day to day. Some rates are controlled by governments, others are free to move according to supply and demand.

foreign investment, the buying of property or securities in a foreign country for investment.

foreign sector, the part of a nation's economy that is concerned with importing foreign goods, exporting home-produced goods, and *foreign investment.

foreman, 1. a worker who is in charge of other workers. **2.** a member of a jury who is spokesman for the others.

forfeited shares, *partly paid shares in a company that a shareholder has to give up because he is unable to pay the balance called for by the company.

forgery, the imitation or alteration of a document, with the intention of trying to pass it off as genuine for the purpose of gain.

formal notice, official notification of something, usually in writing.

forward dating, the dating of a document, cheque, bill of exchange, etc., on some date in the future.

forward dealing, trading in goods or securities for delivery at some date in the future, especially trading on a *futures market.

forward delivery, delivery of goods at some date in the future.

forward exchange, foreign currency bought or sold for delivery at some agreed date in the future.

forwarding agent, a firm that arranges for goods to be delivered from a manufacturer, trader, etc., to the buyer's address, especially when the goods are to be exported. *See also* shipping and forwarding agent.

forward purchases, goods that have been bought for delivery at some agreed date in the future.

forward sales, goods that have been sold for delivery at some agreed date in the future.

foul bill of lading. *See* dirty bill of lading.

founder's shares, shares held by the founders of a company. They often have privileges above those of *ordinary shares.

F.P.A. *See* free of particular average.

franchise, permission to sell or to manufacture a product that has a registered trademark, usually on the basis that the franchise holder pays the owner of the trademark a royalty.

franchise policy, an insurance policy that includes a clause stating that the insured will be responsible for a small stated sum arising from each claim for loss or damage. This eliminates small claims. *See also* excess.

franco (or **rendu**), a contract term denoting that the seller pays all delivery charges to the buyer's warehouse.

franking machine, a machine supplied by a post office to a company to enable the company to frank its own mail. The machine records the value of the stamps used and the company pays for them at the end of a fixed period.

fraud, the use of deception for personal gain. It is usually a criminal offence.

fraudulent conveyance, the act by a person who is bankrupt of signing away property with the intent of defrauding creditors.

fraudulent preference, the act by a person who is bankrupt of giving preference to one creditor over the others.

free alongside ship (F.A.S.), export contract terms in which the seller pays for all the delivery charges to the port of shipment, but not for loading the goods into the ship. He pays for all charges to take the goods to the loading quay or for any *lighter charges.

freeboard, the space between the waterline and the deck on the side of a ship.

free competition, competition between companies without government interference.

free docks, export contract terms in which the seller pays for delivery charges to the docks from which the goods will be shipped.

free economy, an economic system based on *free competition. Prices are controlled only by the market forces of supply and demand.

free entry, the absence of any import duties or import restrictions on a class of goods.

free exchange rate, a rate of currency exchange that is not controlled by a government. It depends only on supply and demand on the *foreign exchange market.

freehold, a form of ownership of land in which the freeholder has absolute possession of the land once he has paid for it.

free list, the list of goods that may be imported into a country without restriction and without paying an import duty.

free market, a commodity market in which prices are determined by supply and demand and traders are free of interference by government regulations of any kind.

free of all averages, a condition in a marine insurance policy that bars the insured for claiming for anything but a total loss. *General average and *particular average claims are thereby excluded.

free of capture, a marine insurance-policy condition that bars the insured from claiming for losses arising from capture of the ship or from mutiny.

free of particular average (F.P.A.), *cargo insurance terms that cover goods against total loss by perils of the sea, fire, or collision. It also includes cover for contributions paid in the event of a *general average. *Compare* with average.

free on board (F.O.B.), export contract terms in which the seller pays for all delivery charges to the port of shipment and for loading them on to the ship. It is the buyer's responsibility to nominate the ship and to cover the marine insurance. These terms can also apply to goods shipped by aircraft.

free on board and trimmed, *free-on-board terms for exporting coal, in which the seller is responsible for seeing that the coal is properly stowed in the ship.

free on quay (F.O.Q.), export contract terms in which the seller is responsible for delivering the goods

free on rail

to the loading quay at the port of shipment, but not for loading them on to the ship.

free on rail (F.O.R.), contract terms in which the seller is responsible for delivering the goods to a railway station or for loading them on to a railway wagon that runs on the main railway network of a country.

free overboard. *See* ex ship.

free port, a port at which goods can be landed and re-exported or transhipped without incurring customs duties.

free sample, a small sample of goods that is representative of the bulk and is given to potential buyers free of charge.

free trade, international trade in which the governments of the countries concerned impose neither import restrictions or duties nor export restrictions.

freeze, a period during which prices (price freeze), wages (wage freeze), or rents (rent freeze) are held at an agreed level for an agreed period in order to combat inflation.

free zone, an area near a port or airport into which goods can be imported free of duty. In this zone they can be manufactured into goods for export or repacked for export.

freight, 1. the transport of goods by land, sea, or air. 2. the cost of transporting a particular lot of goods by ship or by aircraft. It is obtained by multiplying the *freight rate by the weight, volume, or value of the goods. 3. a cargo or shipload of goods.

freight forward, shipping terms in which the freight payable for a shipment is payable at the port of destination.

freight insurance, a clause in a marine insurance policy that covers the insured against the loss of the cost of the freight (in addition to the loss of the goods) in case the ship is lost.

freightliner, a railway train that carries goods in containers.

freight note, the note issued by a shipping company showing the freight charges for a particular shipment.

freight rate, the rate at which freight is charged for a particular voyage for particular goods. Some goods are charged on a weight basis, others on a volume basis, and valuable goods are often charged on an *ad valorem basis.

freight release, an endorsement on a bill of lading authorizing the buyer to take immediate delivery of the goods at the port of destination. The ship-owner or his agents will only endorse the bill of lading in this way if the freight has been paid in advance.

freight ton, a measure of cargo for the purposes of calculating *freight. Formerly it was calculated on the basis of 20 cwt or 40 cubic feet, whichever was the greater. Now it is more commonly calculated on the basis of 1000 kilograms or 1 cubic metre, with separate rates for weight and measurement.

freight train, a train in which goods are transported.

friendly society, an insurance club in which members voluntarily make regular contributions to a fund, from which they can draw in times of illness, old age, etc.

fringe benefit, benefits, such as luncheon vouchers, the right to buy the company's products at a cheap price, pensions, company cars, etc., given to employees in addition to wages or salaries.

frontier, the barrier between one country and another. Part of the frontier may be open but part is usually guarded, with customs posts on roads and at railway stations to check the importation of foreign goods.

frozen assets, assets that cannot easily be converted into liquid money.

frustration, the inability to perform the terms of a contract for reasons that are beyond the control of the contracting parties.

F.T. Index. *See* Financial Times Industrial Ordinary Share Index.

fuel oil, oils, obtained from the distillation of petroleum, that are burnt in ships, domestic boilers, and in diesel engines.

fulfilment, the carrying out of the terms of a contract.

full employment, the state of the labour market in a country when everyone who is willing and able to work has a job.

fully paid shares, shares in a company that have been paid for in full. *Compare* partly paid shares.

fully subscribed, the situation that arises when the whole of a new issue of shares has been applied for by investors. *See* application and allotment.

fund, an amount of money set aside for a particular purpose.

funding operation, the action taken by a government or company to convert a short-term debt, such as an overdraft, into a long-term debt, such as a debenture.

futures market, a *commodity market in which goods are traded in for delivery in the future. This type of market provides a facility for both *hedging and *speculation in commodities with fluctuating prices.

G

galloping inflation, a high rate of *inflation, often assumed to start when prices rise by more than 50% in a month. *Also called* hyperinflation.

gamble, any business venture in which the element of chance predominates.

gaming contract, a contract in which the contracting parties stand to win or lose as the result of a game.

garnishee order, a court order on a person owing money to a *judgment debtor forbidding him to pay the debtor until permitted to do so by the court.

G.D.P. *See* gross domestic product.

gearing, the extent to which the *capitalization of a company is represented by debts, including bank overdrafts and preference-share capital. It is usually expressed as the percentage of such debts to either the total capital or to the shareholder's funds.

general average, partial loss or damage to a ship or its cargo that is incurred as a result of some action for the benefit of the other cargo owners, e.g. throwing some cargo overboard in a storm to save the ship. The resulting *general-average loss* is shared among all the cargo owners and the ship-owners. *Compare* particular average.

general damages, *damages ordered by a court to be paid by one person to another when the loss suffered by the injured party cannot be assessed exactly, e.g. damages for loss of a limb. *Compare* specific damages.

general meeting, a meeting of the members of a company. At least one regular meeting of the members is usually held each year (*see* annual general meeting); other meetings (*see* extraordinary general meeting) may be called by directors or by a stated percentage of the shareholders.

general offer, an offer to sell goods or property to the general public. A person may privately offer to sell his house to another at a certain price and this offer may be restricted to this one buyer. But if he offers the house for sale in a newspaper, this is a general offer that any member of the public may accept.

general partner, a partner in a firm who does not have a limited liability. *Compare* limited partner.

general strike, a strike in which workers in all or most trades withdraw their labour to protest against some government action.

general union, a *trade union comprising all the workers in a country who do not share a common skill (*see* craft union) or do not work in a single industry (*see* industrial union).

gentleman's agreement, an agreement between two or more persons that is not written down and is not enforceable by legal action. It relies on goodwill and trust between the parties.

geometric mean, an average obtained by multiplying together all the quantities to be averaged and taking the nth root of the product, there being n quantities. *Compare* arithmetic mean.

geometric progression, a sequence of numbers in which each term is greater than the one before it by a constant multiple, e.g. 3, 6, 12, 24. *Compare* arithmetic progression.

gift, a transfer of property in which the giver receives no benefit.

gifts tax, a tax on the transfer of property by gift. It is a form of *capital transfer tax.

gill, one-fourth of a pint.

gilt-edged security, a fixed-interest government stock that is considered a safe investment to the extent that a government can be trusted to repay its debts.

giro, a banking system in which debts are settled between customers by transfer from one account to another. In some countries the system is run by the post office.

G.N.P. *See* gross national product.

golden handshake, colloquial name for a payment to a senior executive of a company who is asked to leave before his contract of employment has expired.

gold market, an international market, centred in London and Zurich, on which gold is traded. It has strong links with the currency markets and the price of gold shares on stock exchanges.

gold standard, a monetary system in which the value of a country's currency is pegged to the value of gold.

good, a word used in economics for a commodity or service that is needed by human beings.

goods on approval, goods that a seller is willing to allow a prospective buyer to take to his own premises for a stated period before deciding whether or not he wishes to buy them.

goods on consignment, unsold goods that a principal sends to an agent to sell on his behalf, usually at the best price possible above a certain limit.

goods train, a train that has wagons for transporting goods, etc. *Also called* freight train.

goodwill, the value of a business, such as its reputation and prospects, in excess of the value of its *assets.

go slow, a form of *industrial action in which workers deliberately work at a slower rate than normal.

government bonds, documents issued by a government to members of the public or institutions from whom it borrows money. Government bonds usually pay interest at a fixed rate.

government pension, a pension paid to workers by the government, usually in return for fixed or earnings-related contributions.

government sector, the part of a country's economy that is directly controlled by its government. It includes money raised by taxation, income from nationalized industries and money spent on defence, education, social welfare, etc. *See also* private sector, public sector.

government securities, fixed-interest securities issued by a government to individuals and institutions from whom it borrows money. *Also called* government stocks.

government stocks. *See* government securities.

graft, 1. the abuse of one's position in politics or business for personal profit. **2.** a bribe.

grant of probate, an order authorizing an *executor of a deceased person's will to distribute his property according to the terms of the will.

graph, a diagram in which the relationship between two variable quantities is illustrated by means of continuous lines or curves. Squared paper is often used and the magnitudes associated with various points on the curves are indicated by the

graph paper

scale set out along the axes of the graph.

graph paper, paper on which a graph is drawn; to make the graph easy to plot the paper is usually divided into small squares, which are often contained within larger squares.

gratuity, a tip given to someone, such as a taxi driver or hotel porter, for services rendered. In some occupations gratuities form a major portion of a person's income and are taxable.

graving dock, a dry dock in which ships are repaired, especially if they require maintenance to the hull below the water line.

green pound, the colloquial name for the *unit of account used to calculate Britain's transactions with the Common Market's Community Agricultural Fund.

gross amount, 1. the amount of money showed as owing at the bottom of an invoice, before deduction of discounts, commissions, etc. **2.** the amount earned by a person or business before deduction of expenses, overheads, or taxation.

gross domestic product (G.D.P.), an estimate of the income accruing to the residents of a country and to income generated within the country. *Compare* gross national product.

gross income, a person's income from all sources before deduction of expenses and outgoings. *See also* taxable income, nett income.

gross interest, the total interest from an investment before tax has been deducted. *See also* nett interest.

gross national product (G.N.P.), an estimate of the national income of a country equal to the value of all goods and services produced as well as property income from abroad. *Compare* gross domestic product.

gross profit, 1. the trading profit of a business before deduction of expenses and overheads. **2.** the trading profit of a business after deduction of expenses and overheads but before deduction of taxation. *Also called* pre-tax profit. *See also* nett profit.

gross tonnage, a measurement of the cargo-carrying capacity of a ship equal to the volume of the internal compartments, including all cargo holds. It is expressed in tons of 100 cubic feet. *Also called* gross register tonnage. *See also* nett tonnage.

gross weight, 1. the total weight of a package including the packing material. It is the *nett weight plus the *fare. **2.** the total weight of a road or rail transport vehicle including the goods it is carrying.

ground landlord, the owner of the land on which a *leasehold building stands, to whom *ground rent is paid.

ground rent, money paid annually by the leasehold owner of a building to the *ground landlord upon which it stands.

group life assurance, life assurance policies taken out on a group of people, such as the employees of a business. They sometimes involve reduced premiums and better benefits.

group of companies, a number of companies linked by common ownership. The structure of such groups varies but often consists of one holding company with several subsidiaries.

group relief, a form of tax relief in which the losses of one company in a *group of companies can be set off against the profits of the others for tax purposes.

growth, 1. an increase in the *productivity of a business or nation. **2.** an

guinea

increase in the market value of an asset.

growth stock, ordinary shares in a company whose prospects are thought to be exceptionally good.

guarantee, 1. a type of after-sales service in which a manufacturer undertakes to replace any faulty parts in his product free of charge, for a stated period. **2.** an undertaking by a person to repay a loan made by a bank to some other person, should this other person fail to do so.

guarantor, a person who gives a *guarantee.

guardian, a person entrusted by law to look after the property and interests of a minor or some other person who cannot do so for himself.

guinea, originally a British gold coin made from gold mined in Guinea, and formerly equivalent to 21 shillings; it is now obsolete.

H

haggle, to bargain in an argumentative way.

half-pay, 1. half of full wages or salary. **2.** reduced pay received by officers in the armed services when not actively engaged or appointed to a command.

hallmarks, official marks stamped on articles made of silver, gold, or pewter by Assay offices in the U.K. to indicate a standard of purity. *See also* carat.

handbook, a small book giving guidance on a specific matter, such as instructions for the operation and maintenance of a vehicle or machine.

handling charges, charges made for packing and transporting goods.

harbour, a place either natural or man-made, in which ships can shelter, dock, unload, refuel, etc.

harbour dues, the dues paid by the owners of a ship using the facilities of a *harbour.

harbour master, the person in charge of a *harbour, who regulates the mooring of ships, traffic, etc.

hard currency, a *currency with a relatively high value in comparison to other currencies on the *foreign exchange markets, i.e. one that is in demand but in short supply. *Compare* soft currency.

hard sell, the process of selling goods or services aggressively. *Compare* soft sell.

hardware, 1. goods sold by an ironmonger. **2.** the physical components of a *computer. *Compare* software.

haulage, 1. the carriage of goods by road. **2.** a *carrier's charges for his services, excluding loading or unloading the goods.

haulage contractor, a person who operates a *haulage business.

hazard, a risk or source of danger. In the context of an insurance policy storms, tempest, floods, etc., are called hazards.

head lease, a lease between the owner of a property and a tenant when the tenant has sublet all or part of the property.

health insurance, 1. an insurance policy taken out by a person who can receive payments when by reason of ill-health he is unable to earn money or needs additional funds to pay for his medical treatment. **2.** a government scheme that provides a health service for all the inhabitants of a country.

heavy goods, goods that are manufactured by *heavy industry.

heavy industry, an industry concerned with the manufacture of metals and machinery.

hedging, reducing commercial risktaking, esp. when trading in commodities, by selling goods at the same time as a purchase is made or by buying goods when a sale is made. One of the functions of a *futures market is to enable traders to buy and sell forward so that hedging operations can be carried out.

heir, a person who inherits all or part of the estate of a deceased person.

hereditament, property or land that can be inherited.

hidden reserve, capital reserves that do not appear in the balance sheet

household insurance

of a company. This is an illegal practice if adopted by a *limited company and is usually contrived by undervaluing the assets or overvaluing the liabilities.

hidden tax, any tax that is included in the price of a product and not separately disclosed. For example, duties on alcoholic drink or on tobacco are often not stated at the point of sale.

hidden unemployment, a situation in which people who are employed do not justify the wages they receive because their productivity is so low.

higher education, education beyond secondary education. For example, at a university or polytechnic.

high seas, the sea or seas outside a country's territorial waters.

hire, to use something temporarily in exchange for payment.

hire purchase, an agreement by a person to buy goods and to spread the purchase price over a specified period by paying for the goods in instalments. The buyer is allowed full use of the goods as soon as he has paid the first instalment. All instalments include interest and repayment components.

hire-purchase price, the price of goods paid for by *hire purchase. This will be higher than the *cash price.

hirer, a person who hires something. See hire.

histogram, a statistical graph measuring frequency distributions. It consists of a series of rectangles of variable height and width.

historical-cost accounting, an accounting method in which the original cost of an asset is entered into the books and balance sheet. *Depreciation is charged in the usual way.

hoarding, saving money in preference to spending or investing it.

hogshead, a large cask or barrel of varying capacity but usually containing 54 Imperial gallons of beer.

hold, a cargo space in a ship.

holder, the person in possession of a *bill of exchange at a particular moment.

holder for value, the *holder of a *bill of exchange for which value has been given at some time.

holder in due course, a *holder of a *bill of exchange who has accepted it in good faith for value. In the event that *fraud is involved he still remains as the holder of the bill if he can prove that value was given after the time when the fraud was committed.

holding company, a company controlling other companies by virtue of the fact that it owns more than 50% of the nominal share capital of those companies.

home trade, the internal trade of a country as opposed to the external or export trade.

horizontal integration, the merger of various companies involved in the same stage of the production of a particular product. *Compare* vertical integration.

horizontal mobility, the extent to which people can change jobs, or move to different areas, without change of status. *Compare* vertical mobility.

hot money, money that is transferred from one country to another at short notice in order to make quick profits, for example, to take advantage of high but short-term interest rates, or in anticipation of the devaluation or revaluation of a currency.

household insurance, a form of insurance that covers the risks to a

53

hull insurance

dwelling house and its contents. The risks usually include fire, explosion, storm damage, flood damage, theft, etc.

hull insurance, a marine insurance policy against the risks of a ship foundering or being damaged in a collision, etc. This is separate from the *cargo insurance.

hundredweight (cwt), 1. in the UK, a unit of weight equal to one-twentieth of a ton, or 112 lbs. In the US, a unit of weight equal to 100 lbs (short hundredweight).

hush money, a bribe given to someone to conceal information.

hyperinflation, a high rate of *inflation, often assumed to start when prices rise by more than 50% in a month. *Also called* galloping inflation.

hypermarket, a *supermarket, larger than usual, carrying a wider range of goods.

hypothecation, a letter of authority giving a banker a *lien on goods as security for a loan granted to the shipper of the goods.

I

idle time, time that is not used productively by workers or by machines.

illegal, not allowed by law; unlawful.

illegal partnership, a partnership that is not lawful, usually because it has been formed to carry out an unlawful business or to commit acts that are unlawful.

I.M.F. *See* International Monetary Fund.

immigration, the act of entering a foreign country for the purpose of settling there permanently as a citizen. *Compare* emigration.

imperial preference, a former name for *Commonwealth preference.

Imperial units, units of weights and measures conforming to standards established in the U.K. They include feet, pounds, gallons, etc.

impersonal account, a *ledger account giving details of the assets and capital of a company. *Compare* personal accounts, nominal accounts.

implied terms, the reasonable inferences that can be drawn with regard to the terms of a particular contract. Some terms are not stated but are taken for granted.

import, to bring goods, etc., into a country from outside.

import deposit, a deposit required from importers when their goods arrive in a country. The method is used as an alternative to raising *import duties or to restricting imports.

import duty, a customs duty levied on imported goods at the port of entry. *See also* tariff.

importer, a person or organization that brings goods into a country from another country.

importer's entry form, a form that an *importer has to submit to the customs describing the goods being imported in order that customs duties may be calculated and paid. The goods may not be removed from the port of entry until duty has been paid.

import licence, a licence required by an *importer when his goods are subject to *import quotas or currency controls are in operation.

import quotas, governmental limitations imposed on the import of certain goods. They are usually enforced by requiring the importer to obtain an *import licence.

import restrictions, the restriction of imports to a country by the imposition of *import quotas, *tariffs, or other taxes.

imports, 1. goods imported into a country (*see* visible imports). 2. services, such as shipping, insurance, etc., that earn foreign currency (*see* invisible imports).

import surcharge, an increase temporarily added to a *tariff or *import duty.

imprest account, an advance of money, usually to an official of an organization, to enable him to make sundry payments.

impulse buying, the casual purchase of goods in a shop when the buyer had no previous intention of buying them.

incentive, 1. a motive that stimulates or provokes action. 2. a payment or

inch

concession made to employees to stimulate greater output, better quality work, etc.

inch, a unit of length in the Imperial system. It is equal to one twelfth of a foot or 25·4 millimetres.

incidental expenses, expenses incurred casually in addition to main or regular expenses.

income redistribution, a government taxation policy introduced with the objective of achieving a more equitable distribution of incomes in a community.

incomes policy, a government policy designed to regulate the rate of increase of wages or salaries in an inflationary period.

income tax, tax levied on incomes of individuals. Taxable income is usually arrived at by deducting *income-tax allowances from total income. The rate of tax is usually progressive, increasing as taxable income rises.

income-tax allowances, allowances that are deducted from income before a tax assessment is made. These can be personal allowances, allowances for the upkeep of children or dependants, for life insurance policies, etc.

incorporated company, a company whose legal existence has been formally established by registration with the appropriate government authority. *Articles of Association setting out the objects of the company's activities are required.

increasing returns, an industrial situation in which increases in output are proportionately greater than increases in input. This leads to a reduction in the average cost of production.

increment, an increase or addition, such as a salary increase.

indemnity, an undertaking by one party to give protection to another party for any loss he may suffer. Insurance policies that cover loss or damage to property, goods, etc., are contracts of indemnity.

indenture, a *deed, *contract, or agreement between two or more parties.

indexation, the procedure adopted by governments, employers, or other institutions to increase wages or rates of interest to compensate for the effects of inflation.

index-linked, a salary, wage, or price that is subject to *indexation.

indirect costs, the costs of producing goods, such as maintenance, rent, administration, etc., that do not vary with output. *Also called* fixed costs, overheads, oncosts.

indirect labour, those workers not directly engaged in production but who provide ancillary services, such as office work, etc.

indirect taxation, taxation that is not levied on a person's income but on goods that he purchases, such as petrol, consumer goods, cars, etc.

industrial action, any activity by a work force taken to further its claims for higher pay or better *working conditions. It includes *strikes, *working to rule, etc.

industrial dispute, a dispute between workers and management in a company. It can arise through workers' dissatisfaction with conditions of service, rates of pay, wrongful dismissal, etc.

industrial espionage, an attempt by a person to discover the commercial secrets or processes of a company in order to convey the information to another company.

industrial estate, an area, set aside from the residential part of a town, in which factories, workshops, ware-

instalment plan

houses, etc., are built. They may be owned outright or leased from the government or a local authority. *Also called* trading estate.

industrialist, the owner of an industrial enterprise.

industrial market research. *See* market research.

industrial nations, the European countries, America, Russia, and Japan. *Compare* developing countries.

industrial union, a *trade union comprising all the workers in a single plant or a particular industry. Qualification for entry does not depend on possession of a particular skill, as in a *craft union. *See also* general union.

industry, a large-scale business activity, especially a branch of trade or manufacture, such as the *oil industry* or the *tourist industry.*

infant, (in law) a person under the age of 18.

inflation, an economic situation in which a decline in the purchasing value of a currency leads to increasing prices and increasing wage demands.

inflationary spiral, an economic situation in which price rises lead to successful demands for increased wages, which in turn lead to further price rises and further wage demands.

informative advertising, the form of *advertising that assists prospective buyers to choose between alternative products. *Compare* persuasive advertising.

infringement of copyright, the act of publishing something that is covered by someone else's *copyright.

ingot, a precious metal, such as gold or silver, cast into the form of a bar.

inherent vice, a characteristic of certain goods such as the inflammability of petrol, that makes them dangerous to transport and therefore expensive to insure.

inheritance, property that passes to an heir on the death of the owner.

inheritance tax, a tax paid by an heir on the value of his *inheritance.

injunction, a court order requiring a person to perform (or not perform) some action.

injured party, the party in a legal action who has received some harm or has been wronged.

injury, harm, wrong, or injustice caused by the deliberate or negligent act of someone. Redress for an injury can be sought in a court of law.

inquiry, 1. an investigation into some matter, especially an official investigation as in a *Court of Inquiry.* **2.** a request for a quotation or offer for a product, security, etc. *Also* enquiry.

inscribed stock, government *stocks for which certificates are not issued but holders' names are inscribed in a register. *Also called* registered stock.

insider, a person with access to confidential information that could affect the price of the shares in a company.

insolvency, the condition in which a person or company is unable to pay its outstanding debts. If the person or company has no liquid assets this will lead to *bankruptcy.

inspector of taxes, a person employed by a government department who is responsible for assessing the tax due by a person or by a company. *Compare* collector of taxes.

instalment plan, an agreement to purchase goods by paying for them in regular instalments, which usually include interest. *See also* hire purchase.

instant

instant, of this month, often abbreviated to *inst.* E.g. 24th inst. refers to the 24th of this month. *Compare* proximo, ultimo.

institute cargo clauses, cargo insurance clauses devised by the Institute of London Underwriters for use in marine insurance policies.

institutional investors, institutions, such as banks, pension fund investment trusts, insurance companies, etc., that invest capital and income in securities.

insurable interest, a commercial interest held by a person in the subject of an insurance policy. The possession of an insurable interest is necessary to make an insurance policy legal.

insurance, a method of providing a person, company, etc., with compensation for unpredictable losses or misfortunes. The insured pays regular premiums to the insurer: should the insured suffer a loss as a result of the risk against which he has insured, he makes a claim on the insurer, who pays the compensation out of the fund built up from all the premiums he has collected. *Compare* assurance.

insurance agent, a person who acts for an insurance company by obtaining customers. He usually follows some other profession of his own, such as banking, which brings him into contact with people needing insurance cover.

insurance broker, a person who negotiates with insurance companies or underwriters on behalf of people wishing to insure against various risks. He usually receives a commission from the insurers and is an expert adviser seeking the best terms for his clients.

insurance certificate, a document certifying that the holder is insured against some risk. The terms of the insurance are set out in the insurance policy: the certificate is to prove that the holder is covered by insurance.

insurance claim, a claim made by the holder of an insurance policy to compensate him from a loss that he has suffered, as agreed in the terms of the policy.

insurance company, a company that, in exchange for agreed premiums, will compensate a policy holder for specified losses, should they occur.

insurance cover, the protection enjoyed by a person who has taken out an insurance policy against some specified risk.

insurance policy, a document stating the terms under which *insurance cover has been provided by an insurer.

insurance premium, the payment made by an insured party to the insurer for a particular *insurance cover. It may be a lump sum or a regular annual or monthly payment.

insured, a person, company, etc., who pays a premium to an *insurer to obtain *insurance cover.

insurer, an insurance company, underwriter, or other party who charges a premium to provide an *insured with *insurance cover.

intangible assets, assets, such as goodwill or a well-known trademark, that have no easily identifiable financial value but that add to the reputation and market value of a company. *Compare* tangible assets.

intelligent terminal, a computer input or output device that can itself carry out some processing of data.

interest, a payment made for borrowing money, usually expressed as a percentage of the capital sum borrowed. *See also* compound interest, simple interest.

interest rate, the annual rate of interest charged on money borrowed.

interim dividend, any distribution of profits in the form of a *dividend to shareholders, except for the *final dividend, made by a company in a particular year. If there is more than one such dividend they are known as the first interim dividend, second interim dividend, etc.

interim report, a statement by a company, whose shares are available for purchase on a stock exchange, regarding the trading results attained during the first six months of its financial year.

internal audit, the audit of a company's accounts by its own accountants for control purposes. This is in contrast to an audit made by an outside firm of accountants for statutory purposes.

International Bank for Reconstruction and Development. *See* World Bank Group.

International Development Association. *See* World Bank Group.

International Finance Corporation. *See* World Bank Group.

International Monetary Fund (I.M.F.), a fund set up in 1947 by the United Nations to promote international cooperation in monetary affairs, to stabilize exchange rates, to help in the expansion of world trade, and to provide funds to enable countries with *balance of payment problems to maintain the value of their currencies. Its headquarters are in Washington.

intestacy, the state of a person's affairs if he dies without having made a will.

intrinsic value, the value of something before it has been transformed into a marketable product.

inventory, a list of materials, stocks, components, spare parts, etc., held by a company or organization.

investment, 1. the expenditure of money to buy capital goods, such as factory machinery, to increase the production of a factory. **2.** the purchase of securities to earn income and sometimes to obtain capital growth.

investment analyst, an expert in forecasting the prices of securities, usually by analysing the past and present performance of companies and their trading results.

investment bank, a bank that finances and promotes the sale of new share issues.

investment club, a group of investors who pool their resources to buy securities on a scale that they would be unable to do individually.

investment grant, a grant to a company made by a government to encourage the purchase of more up-to-date machinery, thus improving production.

investment incentives, government incentives, such as *investment grants, taxation relief, subsidies of various kinds, to encourage industries to increase their investment in capital equipment.

investment income, income derived from investments. *See also* unearned income.

investment portfolio, a list of the investments held by a person or an organization.

investment trust, a company that buys and sells securities and offers its own shares for sale to investors. The aim is to allow a small investor to spread his investments over many securities, thus reducing the risk of loss. *Unit trusts are also investment trusts, but the investor is not a shareholder in this case.

investor, a person who invests money in an enterprise or in securities in order to make a profit.

invisible assets. *See* intangible assets.

invisibles, services, such as insurance, shipping, etc., that earn or cost foreign exchange. Invisibles enter into a country's *balance of payments but not its *balance of trade. *Compare* visibles.

invitation to treat, a request to someone to discuss making an offer for goods. Acceptance of the offer would constitute a contract.

invoice, a document demanding payment for goods or services. It provides details of the goods or services and shows how the total amount owing is made up. It may also give details of delivery, payment terms, and insurance cover in transit.

invoice discounting. *See* factor.

I.O.U., abbreviation for "I owe you". It constitutes a written acknowledgement of a debt.

irredeemable debenture, a *debenture that cannot be redeemed but is purchased solely for the interest payments.

irredeemable security, a security, such as certain government stocks and ordinary shares, that have no *redemption date. *Also called* undated security.

irrevocable letter of credit, a *letter of credit that cannot be cancelled before the expiry date without the consent of the beneficiary or the issuing bank. *Compare* revocable letter of credit.

issue, 1. the number of *shares in a company offered for sale to the public. **2.** the number of banknotes printed at one time.

issue by tender, an issue of shares in which the public is invited to *tender for their purchase, the shares being issued to the highest bidders.

issued capital, the amount of a company's *capital that is issued to shareholders.

issue price, the price at which a security is issued. This is not necessarily the same as its *face value. If the issue price is higher than the denomination of the security (face value) it is said to be issued at a premium over its *par value. If it is lower, it is at a discount to its par value.

issuing house, a bank or finance house that underwrites a new issue of *shares and sells them to the public.

J, K

jerque, to search a ship to check that it contains no cargo that has been omitted from the captain's list submitted to the customs.

jetsam, goods thrown overboard to lighten a ship in distress. *See also* flotsam and jetsam.

jettisons, a marine insurance term for goods thrown overboard to save a ship in distress. If the goods form part of an insured cargo they constitute a *general average loss.

jetty, a wharf or landing pier in a harbour or river.

job, 1. the work upon which a person is employed. 2. an individual piece of work.

jobber, 1. a dealer in stocks and shares. He does not sell to the public direct but does so through a *stockbroker. *Also called* stockjobber. 2. any dealer in special or job lots.

jobber's turn, the profit sought by a stockjobber through the purchase and sale of stocks and shares. The jobber's turn is the difference between the price that he is prepared to pay and the price at which he is prepared to sell.

jobbing backwards, realizing that in the light of subsequent information one's past decisions could have been made differently and more profitably.

job costing, the type of costing in which costs are recorded against each individual job or order to assess the *profitability of various types of jobs.

job evaluation, an assessment of the skill and experience needed to perform a particular job in order to assess its value in terms of wages or salaries.

job-knowledge tests, tests of a person's skill, experience, and suitability for a particular job.

joint account, a bank account in the names of two or more persons (often husband and wife) from which withdrawals may be made by any one of the parties.

joint and several liability, responsibility by each one of the guarantors for the full amount of a debt, when the debt has been guaranteed jointly by two or more guarantors.

joint life and last survivor annuities, an *annuity providing a higher income for a husband and wife while they are both living but which falls to a half or two-thirds on the death of one of them.

joint-stock bank, a bank that is a public *limited company. *Compare* private bank.

joint tenants, two or more people who jointly own a property. If one of them should die the remaining tenants divide his share equally between them.

journal, a book of account in which all transactions are recorded day by day before being posted to the appropriate ledger.

judgment creditor, a person who has proved in court that he is owed money by another person.

judgment debtor, a person who has been ordered by a court to pay a debt to another.

judgment summons, the legal process used to procure the committal of a

junior partner

*judgment debtor who has failed to pay his debt as ordered by the court.

junior partner, a partner in a business who is entitled to a smaller share of the profits than the other partner or partners.

kaffirs, a colloquial name for South African gold-mining shares.

keelage, fees paid by a ship entering and staying in certain ports.

key industry, an industry that is vital to the economy of a country.

key money, a premium paid to obtain a lease of a residential property, often charged on long leases where the rent is below market value or when such properties are scarce.

key worker, a skilled worker who is able to train other employees and organize the installation of plant, machinery, etc.

kite, a colloquial name for an *accommodation bill.

kite mark, the symbol used by the *British Standards Institution to indicate that a product meets its standards.

knock-for-knock agreement, an agreement between insurance companies that underwrite motor-car insurance not to attempt to establish responsibility for an accident. Each company pays for the repair or replacement of its own policyholder's vehicle in accordance with the terms of the policy.

knot, one nautical mile per hour. It is equal to approximately 1·15 miles per hour.

L

labor union, the U.S. name for a *trade union.

labour force, 1. the workers employed in a particular industry or by a particular company. **2.** all the workers in a country.

labour-intensive industry, an industry in which the costs of employing *labour are high relative to the costs of equipment, machinery, etc. *Compare* capital-intensive industry.

labour market, the market that determines what workers are available for different kinds of job and what they should be paid.

laissez-faire, the economic theory that governments should intervene as little as possible in economic affairs.

Lancashire flat, a platform upon which containers can be placed to enable them to be hoisted on to lorries or ships.

land bank, 1. a bank that grants long-term loans to finance agricultural development of land. **2.** the land held in reserve by a developer.

land certificate, a certificate issued by a land registry to the owner of registered land.

landed, export contract terms in which the exporter pays for shipping the goods to their port of destination and for landing them from the vessel on to the quay. He does not pay the cost of delivering from the quay.

landing account, a document issued by a warehousing company listing the goods that have recently been landed from a ship for a particular buyer. It shows the cost of unloading the goods and any rent that has been incurred.

landlord, 1. the owner of land. **2.** a person who leases land, living accommodation, offices, factories, etc., to another.

land registration, a system used in the U.K. to aid the process of transferring the ownership of land. Each piece of land is registered and the owner has a certificate proving registration.

language laboratory, a special school for teaching businessmen, students, etc., to speak a foreign language. It is usually based on tape-recorded conversations supervised by an instructor.

larboard, the left-hand side of a ship looking forward. Now generally superseded by the word *port* to avoid confusion with the starboard (right-hand) side.

larceny, the unlawful taking of someone's goods or property with the intention of using them oneself.

LASH. *See* lighter aboard ship.

last in, first out (LIFO), a method of valuing the stock of raw materials of a business based on the assumption that the stock to be used first was the last to arrive. This method makes the remaining stock cheap in times of inflation. *Compare* first in, first out.

latent defect, a concealed, hidden, or invisible defect in something.

lawyer, a *solicitor or *barrister engaged in the legal profession.

lay days, the customary number of days allowed for loading or unload-

lay-off

ing a ship. If exceeded, *demurrage can be charged to the ship-owner.

lay-off, the temporary suspension of workers by a company, often because necessary components are not available because of a strike in another factory.

lay-off pay, the U.S. name for redundancy pay.

lease, 1. an agreement or *contract in which the owner of a property lets it to another person, in exchange for rent, for a specified period. **2.** the period of time for which a lease is made.

lease-back, an arrangement in which land or property is sold on condition that the seller can lease the land or property back for a specified period by paying an agreed rent. For example, a company may erect new offices for its own use and on completion of the building sell it to recover the capital outlay but immediately lease the building back and pay rent for its use. Thus the capital is available for other purposes.

leasehold land, land leased to a person who pays *ground rent to the *freeholder of the land.

ledger, a book of account used in *double-entry book-keeping. It may be separated into several books of account, such as the sales ledger, purchase ledger, etc.

ledger clerk, a person responsible for keeping the *ledger up-to-date by recording entries in it daily.

legal action, an action at law leading to civil or criminal proceedings in a court of law.

legal liability, any responsibility or obligation that is enforceable by law.

legal reserve, the fund of money that insurance companies, banks, building societies, etc., are required by law to maintain in reserve, as security for their customers.

lender of last resort, the central bank in a country that will lend to the commercial banks when they need to borrow.

lessee, a person to whom a *lease is granted.

lessor, a person who grants a *lease to another.

letterhead, the name and address and other details regarding a company that are printed on its stationery.

letter of allotment, the document informing an applicant of the number of shares allotted to him after he has applied for a *new issue of shares.

letter of credit, an instruction from a banker to a foreign bank or agent authorizing the payment of money to the person named in the letter.

letter of hypothecation, a pledge to a banker, in exchange for credit, by an exporter or shipper authorizing him to sell the goods pledged, if the buyer of the goods issues a *bill of exchange that is not paid.

letter of indemnity, a letter written by an exporter of goods that accompanies the shipping documents. It states that the exporter will make good any losses through faulty packing or short weight at the time of loading the goods on to a ship. In return the shipping company will usually issue a *clean bill of lading.

letter of licence, a letter written by creditors to a debtor giving him a specified time in whch to pay before legal proceedings are taken to enforce payment. A letter of licence, officially registered, is binding on the creditor.

letter of regret, a letter sent to an applicant for a *new issue of shares, job, etc., informing him that his application has been unsuccessful.

liquidated damages

letter of renunciation, a letter from a shareholder renouncing his right to the shares allotted to him.

letters of administration, an order by a court of law appointing an administrator to distribute the estate of a deceased person, who has failed to appoint someone in his will to perform this function.

letters patent, an official document granting a *patent to an inventor and conferring upon him, for a specified period, the exclusive right to make, use, and sell his invention.

levy, a tax or duty. *See also* capital levy.

liability, an obligation or a debt. *See also* current liabilities, contingent liabilities, deferred liabilities, long-term liabilities.

liability insurance, a form of insurance providing cover for damages and costs awarded to a *third party, who has suffered loss or injury for which the policy holder is liable.

licence, a certificate of permission issued by an authority to allow the holder the legal right to something. For example, to drive a car, possess firearms, etc.

lien, a legal right to hold the goods or property of another person, who is in debt to the holder.

life assurance, 1. an insurance policy providing payment of a specified sum of money to the estate of the policy holder or to a named beneficiary, on his death. **2.** a similar policy providing for payment to the holder should he survive to a specified age.

life interest, a share in property or commercial undertakings held by a person during his lifetime.

LIFO. *See* last in, first out.

lighter, an unpowered vessel used for conveying cargo to or from ships in harbours or rivers. It is towed by a tug or other vessel.

lighter aboard ship (LASH), a rapid method of cargo handling using a *lighter that can be lifted bodily by a crane on to a ship's deck.

lighterage, the fees paid for the use of a *lighter.

limit, a restriction on the price that a buyer of securities or commodities will pay or that a seller will sell at.

limited company, a company, whether public or private, in which the liability of a shareholder is limited to the nominal value of his shares.

limited letter of credit, a *letter of credit issued by a bank authorizing its agents in a limited number of places only to make payments to a customer. *Compare* circular letter of credit.

limited liability. *See* limited company, limited partner.

limited partner, a partner in a firm whose liability for debts is limited to the amount of capital he has invested in the firm. *Compare* general partner.

limit-pricing, commercial tactics adopted to discourage competitors by lowering prices and increasing output. These tactics can only be maintained for limited periods.

liner, a passenger and cargo ship owned by a shipping line and operating on a fixed itinerary. *Compare* tramp steamer.

liquid assets, the *assets of a company or person, such as money in the bank or bonds, that can easily be converted into cash.

liquidated damages, an agreed amount to be paid as compensation should a party to a *contract fail to fulfill his obligations to the other party. The sum is agreed at the time the contract is made.

liquidation

liquidation, the closing-down of a company either voluntarily or because a court has declared the company to be insolvent. *See* voluntary liquidation, compulsory liquidation.

liquidator, a person appointed by the members of a company, by its creditors, or by a court, to administer the *liquidation of a company. Initially, he may be the *official receiver. His duties are to realize the assets of the company and distribute the proceeds to the creditors.

liquidity, the proportion of *liquid assets to other assets held by a person or company. The higher the proportion of liquid assets the higher its liquidity.

list price, the published price of a product; the price that the consumer expects to pay for it. In a time of *recession the *retailer may offer a product below list price by reducing his own commission.

livestock and bloodstock insurance, the insurance of cattle, horses, and other animals against the risk of death or disease, etc.

Lloyd's, an association of insurance *underwriters in the City of London, concerned largely with marine insurance but also with various other forms of insurance. Lloyd's underwriters, organized into syndicates, individually underwrite the risks and Lloyd's brokers obtain the business from the public.

Lloyd's broker, an insurance *broker who obtains business for *Lloyd's underwriters.

Lloyd's register of shipping, an organization formed by *Lloyd's to survey and classify all vessels of 100 tons or more and to publish annually details of these ships in the *Lloyd's Register of British and Foreign Shipping*.

Lloyd's underwriter, a member of *Lloyd's, who transacts insurance business on his own account. Underwriters join syndicates to share the risks involved, particularly with shipping. They deal with the public only through a *Lloyd's broker.

load line, a line running around a ship to indicate the maximum extent to which it may be immersed. *Also called* Plimsoll line.

loan, a sum of money lent to someone, usually in return for *interest.

loan account, an account opened by a bank for a client who wishes to borrow a fixed sum from the bank. The full amount of the loan is debited to this account and credited to the client's *current account. The loan is usually repayable over a fixed period at a fixed rate, often by regularly debiting the client's current account with amounts made up partly of loan interest and partly of repayments.

loan stock. *See* debenture.

lock-out, the refusal by an employer to allow his employees to enter his premises or factory during the course of an industrial dispute.

lock-up, 1. rented storage space that can be locked up for security. **2.** a long-term investment.

long-dated gilt, a *gilt-edged security that cannot be redeemed for 15 years or more.

long position, the state of a speculator in securities or commodities, who has purchased more than he has sold in anticipation of a market rise.

longs, 1. short for *long-dated gilts. **2.** goods or securities bought to establish a *long position.

long-term capital, capital borrowed by a company to finance long-term capital projects. This will be made up of long-term loans, *debentures,

luxury goods

etc., as opposed to such short-term loans as *overdrafts.

long-term liability, a loan, shown on a *balance sheet, that does not have to be repaid in the current year. In some contexts a long-term liability does not have to be paid for three years.

long ton, a unit of weight equal to 2240 lbs or 1016 kilograms. It is now being replaced in the U.K. by the *tonne* (or metric ton) of 1000 kilograms.

loss, 1. failure to recover costs in a commercial operation. **2.** the liability incurred by an insurer when the insured makes a valid claim.

loss leader, goods sold at a loss or at a reduced profit in order to attract customers who may then buy other goods.

loss-of-profit policies. *See* consequential loss policies.

loss ratio, the ratio of the total premiums paid to an insurance company to the total paid out in claims.

Ltd. abbreviation for limited. *See* limited company.

lump sum, 1. a sum of money paid all at one time, either in addition to or in place of a series of periodic payments. For example, a widow might receive a lump sum from her late husband's employers, in place of a pension or an annuity. **2.** a sum of money paid for *freight that is not dependent on the amount of goods shipped.

lump-sum tax, a tax levied as a fixed amount rather than as a proportion of income, profits, etc.

lump system, a system of paying workers, particularly in the building industry, in which they receive lump sums daily for work done. They are not directly employed but are regarded as sub-contractors. The system arose to enable such workers to avoid paying income-tax.

luncheon voucher, a voucher for a fixed small amount, issued by employers to their employees, to enable them to buy meals at certain restaurants, cafés, etc. This system is usually adopted by firms that do not have canteen facilities.

Lutine bell, a bell recovered from the wreck of the ship *Lutine* that hangs in the underwriting room at *Lloyd's and is rung when important news affecting the insurance market is announced.

luxury goods, articles of merchandise that are expensive to purchase and are not essential to everyday life.

M

machine-down time, the time during which a machine is out of action because it is being serviced or repaired.

machine-idle time, the time during which a machine is out of action because of a shortage of labour, raw materials, or orders for finished products.

machine language, the language used to input data into a computer.

macroeconomics, the study and analysis of an economy as a whole. It is concerned with the interaction of such factors as production, and demand, unemployment, prices, money supply, the rate of inflation, taxation, etc. *Compare* *microeconomics.

mail order, a method of marketing in which goods are sold using the postal services to advertise the products, solicit orders, and make deliveries.

mail transfer, the transfer of money using the postal services.

majority holding, a person or organization that holds more than 50% of the nominal share capital of a company.

management, the persons responsible for the control, direction, and coordination of an organization, business, or company.

management accountant, an accountant who analyses the financial affairs of a company, including its running costs, in order to advise the *management and to assist them in making decisions affecting the business.

management consultant, an expert in the techniques of business management, whose services can be sought by a company to investigate a particular aspect of its activities, with the object of improving efficiency.

manager, a person in charge of a department of a business who performs the functions of *management.

managing director, the director of a company who is responsible for the day-to-day *management of the company. In a very large company there may be more than one managing director, each with a different area of responsibility.

mandate, a written order signed by a person giving another person authority to act on his behalf.

man-hour, the amount of work that a man can complete in one hour.

manifest, a list of a ship's cargo, certified by the captain, for the information of the *customs.

manpower, the number of people available to work in a particular area, industry, or country. It includes women.

manufacturer, a person who owns or operates a plant making goods, especially *consumer goods.

manufacturer's agent, an agent licensed by a *manufacturer to market his goods in a particular area on commission.

margin, 1. the difference between the cost price and the selling price of goods, securities, etc. **2.** the deposit paid to a *broker by an investor or speculator to cover any possible losses that he may make.

marine insurance, insurance covering risks to ships, passengers, cargo, and freight.

market, 1. a gathering of people for the purpose of trading. **2.** the place in which such trading is carried on. **3.** the demand or estimated demand for a commodity, security, or service.

marketable, readily saleable.

marketable security, a *security for which there is a *market.

market assessment, the identification and evaluation of a market for a company's or an industry's goods.

market capitalization, an assessment of the market value of a company obtained by multiplying the total number of issued shares by the market price of the shares.

market forces, the factors that influence a market for goods, etc., particularly *supply and demand.

marketing, the process of investigating whether or not a *market exists for particular goods, services, etc., and of pricing and selling them. *See also* market assessment, market research.

market leader, a company with the largest share of a *market by virtue of the fact that its products are very competitive through price, quality, or a combination of both.

market penetration, the measure of a company's success in selling a particular product, expressed as the proportion of all sales of that type of product captured by the company. It is often given as a percentage.

market price, the price at which a product, security, or service sells in the open market.

market research, investigation of a market, by surveys, etc., to assess its size for a particular consumer product (consumer research) or industrial product (industrial market research). *Compare* marketing.

market share, the percentage of the total sales of a particular product that are made by one company.

market value, 1. an estimate of the value of goods or property if it were to be sold on the open market. **2.** the current value of a security on a stock exchange.

mark-up, the percentage added to the cost of a product when fixing its selling price.

mass production, the manufacture of products in large quantities by mechanical means, usually involving an assembly line in which components are added to a basic framework.

master, a ship's captain.

mate, an officer in a merchant ship ranking below the master or captain.

material fact, a fact that may affect the risk taken by an insurance underwriter in granting an insurance policy. For example, the health of the assured person is material in the case of an application for life assurance.

mate's receipt, a written acknowledgement by the *mate of a ship that a specific cargo has been loaded into the ship.

maturity, 1. the date on which a *bill of exchange becomes payable for cash. **2.** the date on which an insurance policy becomes payable to the holder (i.e. exchanged for cash after an agreed term).

mean, 1. the average value of a set of values. **2.** *See* geometric mean.

mean price, the average price, often the average between the seller's asking price and the buyer's bidding price of a security or commodity. It is sometimes taken as the market price.

means test, an investigation of the means, or resources, of a person claiming social security benefits or other welfare benefits.

measurement tonnage, a measure of the cargo-carrying capacity of a ship, expressed as the *gross tonnage or the *nett tonnage in tons of 100 cubic feet.

mechanical engineer, a person qualified to design and construct or to maintain engines, machinery, etc.

mechanization, the introduction of machines in industry, agriculture, etc., to replace manual labour.

media, the means of communicating with the public for the purposes of advertising, providing information, etc. It usually refers to newspapers, radio, and television.

medical insurance, insurance taken out by a person to cover the costs of hospital accommodation and medical treatment should this become necessary.

medium-dated gilt, a *gilt-edged security that can be redeemed in between five and 15 years.

meeting of creditors, during proceedings against a person who has been declared *bankrupt, his creditors meet to decide whether or not to come to some arrangement with him regarding his debts or to accept whatever share of his assets the trustee appointed by the court may apportion to them.

memorandum of association, a document drawn up when a company is formed that defines the objects and powers of the company and its directors. It states the authorized capital of the company and lists the number of shares held by each founder member.

mercantile agent, an agent authorized to buy or sell goods on behalf of another person.

mercantile law, 1. the various laws governing trading practices in a country. **2.** the laws controlling international trade and shipping.

merchandise, saleable goods or products.

merchandising, sales promotion involving such techniques as *advertising, sales campaigns, etc.

merchant, a trader who buys and sells commodities for his own account, rather than as a *broker or *agent.

merchantable quality, goods that are free of defects and of acceptable quality to a reasonable person.

merchant bank, a bank that, unlike a *joint stock bank, is concerned with financing trading enterprises rather than providing a service for the general public. They often deal in foreign exchange, provide long-term loan facilities for private companies, and underwrite new share issues.

merchant ship, a ship engaged in the transport of goods.

merger, the amalgamation of two or more companies to form one new company usually in the interests of increased efficiency.

metrication, the process of changing from a non-metric system of measurements to a *metric system.

metric system, a decimal system of measuring weights, distances, etc. *SI units are now the internationally accepted units for scientific and technical purposes. This is a metric system based on the metre and kilogram.

metric ton, a unit of weight equal to 1000 kilograms (2204·6 lbs). *Also called* tonne.

metrology, the science of weights and measures.

microeconomics, the study and analysis of the economic factors affecting individuals or individual companies. *Compare* macroeconomics.

microfiche, a small sheet of film

microfilm, a roll of film containing reduced images of documents, etc., for storage purposes. To read the image a viewer has to be used.

middleman, an intermediary through whose hands a product passes between the producer and the consumer. He often provides finance or a distribution network for the producer.

middle price, the average price of a security on a *stock exchange. It is half way between the bid price and the offer price.

mineral, an inorganic substance or ore, usually obtained from a mine and used as a source of a metal or other useful element.

mineral concession, permission granted by a government or controlling authority to a person or company to dig for *minerals in a specified place under agreed conditions, usually including the payment of royalties to the authority.

mineral rights, the rights to extract minerals from the earth in a particular area, usually from land that is owned by someone else.

minimum lending rate (M.L.R.), a rate of interest published by the Bank of England indicating the minimum rate at which it will discount *bills of exchange maturing within three months, or grant short-term loans in its capacity as a *lender of last resort.

minimum wage, the lowest wage that an employer can pay to an employee for a specific job. In some countries, such as the U.S. and Canada, minimum wages are prescribed by law.

minor, a young person who has not reached the age of legal responsibility.

minority interest, a person or firm that owns less than 50% of the shares in a company and can therefore be outvoted at a shareholder's meeting.

mint, a government factory in which coins and banknotes are manufactured.

minutes, a note recording the proceedings of a meeting.

misfeasance summons, a writ issued by a court of law calling upon a person to appear before the court to answer charges of wrongly using the authority vested in him. The procedure is commonly used when companies are being wound up in order to obtain judgement against an official of the company.

misrepresentation, an act in which one person persuades another to enter into a *contract but conceals or falsifies information relevant to the terms of the contract (fraudulent misrepresentation). Innocent misrepresentation occurs if a genuine mistake has been made. In both cases damages can be obtained and the contract rescinded by a court.

mitigation of damage, the reduction of damages claimed by a person who has suffered loss through breach of *contract if, in the opinion of a court, he has not taken all the steps necessary to minimize the damage.

mixed economy, an economy in which private enterprise and state enterprise (i.e. nationalized industries) exist alongside one another.

M.L.R. *See* minimum lending rate.

mock auction, an illegal auction in which the laws regarding the conduct of auctions have been evaded. For example, when a lot is sold at a price lower than one that is bid.

monetary policy

monetary policy, the policy of a government regarding the amount of money in circulation. The control of the money supply can lead to inflation if too much money is in circulation, or to recession and unemployment if there is too little.

monetary reform, a change in the currency of a country when, for example, it is revalued, or when new units of currency are introduced, as in the case of decimalization.

monetary system, the arrangements made in a country with regard to its currency: the units used, the value given to the units in relation to the currencies of other countries, the capital reserves required to maintain the value of the currency in the foreign exchange market, etc.

money, the medium of exchange, consisting of coins and banknotes.

money broker, an intermediary working on commission who deals in short-term loans, securities, etc., on a *money market.

moneylender, a person who is licensed to lend money. In many countries a maximum rate of interest must not be exceeded by law. In the U.K., for example, it must not exceed 48%.

money market, the market for lending or borrowing money at call or at short notice. The *foreign exchange market and the bulletin market are often regarded as part of the money market.

money wages, wages in terms of money without taking into account the purchasing power of the money. *Compare* real wages.

monopoly, 1. a situation in which the market in a particular product is controlled by one person, or a group of people acting together, enabling them to obtain artificially high prices for their product. 2. an industry with only one producer and many consumers.

monthly instalment, an arrangement in which a purchaser of goods can pay for them by equal monthly sums for a fixed period. The total paid will include an interest payment. *See also* hire purchase.

moonlighting, a colloquial name for casual work done by a person, after he has finished his normal day's employment, to enable him to earn additional money.

moratorium, an officially authorized period during which the obligation to pay debts is suspended.

mortality rate, the number of deaths that have ocurred per 1000 of the population in one year.

mortgage, a deed conditionally conveying a property to someone in exchange for a promise to repay (with interest) a loan made to purchase the property. The property is the security for the loan until it has been repaid.

mortgage debenture, a deed containing a *mortgage on a company's assets, enabling the company to raise loan capital.

mortgagee, a person who lends money on *mortgage.

mortgagor, a person who borrows money on a *mortgage.

motion, a proposal formally put to a meeting. If accepted by the majority of the members present, the motion will be adopted and the necessary action taken.

motivational research, a study of the motivation of a consumer who buys one product in preference to a similar product.

motor insurance, 1. third-party insurance: insurance required by law in most countries to cover a motorist's liability towards passen-

mutual life assurance company

gers, owners and occupants of other vehicles, pedestrians, etc., who may suffer injury or loss as a result of his actions. 2. comprehensive insurance: insurance covering all risks to the driver, his vehicle, and to third parties.

mountain, a stockpile of surplus produce, usually agricultural produce that accumulates due to overproduction or to some protectionist measure, such as the Common Agricultural Policy of the European Economic Community.

moveable assets, articles of personal property not attached to land.

multilateral trade, trading between many countries.

multinational, a large company owning subsidiary companies in several countries.

municipal, pertaining to the local government of a town.

mutual funds, the U.S. name for *unit trusts.

mutual life assurance company, an insurance company whose funds are derived from members' contributions. There are no shareholders and the fund is used only to pay running expenses and benefits.

N

name, a member of a *Lloyd's underwriting syndicate.

national banks, banks in the U.S. established under federal law, as opposed to state banks established under state laws.

national debt, the debts incurred by a government as a result of borrowing money internally or from foreign sources.

national income, the value of all goods and services produced by a country during a specified period of time, less capital consumption. If capital consumption is included then the national income is described as *gross national product (G.N.P.).

nationalization, the process of bringing a firm or industry under direct state control and ownership.

nationalized industry, an industry that has been subject to *nationalization.

national plan, an official plan introduced by a government for the economic development of the country over a specified period.

natural gas, a mixture of gases, predominantly methane, that occurs in the earth especially above oil deposits. It is used as a fuel.

nautical mile, a distance of 6080 feet or 1·85 km.

navigable waters, canals, rivers, estuaries, etc., that can be traversed by shipping.

negligence, failure to carry out a duty or obligation through lack of care. In certain cases, a person who has suffered from a negligent act may be able to claim damages by taking legal action.

negotiability, the capacity of a document, such as a *bill of exchange or a cheque, to be transferred to another person. *See also* endorsement.

negotiation, any discussion aimed at reaching an agreement, especially a discussion that leads to the conclusion of a business deal or an agreement between a union and management.

nett assets, the working capital of a company, represented by the difference between current assets and current liabilites.

nett book amount, the value of an asset as it appears in a company's books, after deducting *depreciation.

nett domestic product, the *gross domestic product excluding capital consumption.

nett income, a person's income after paying all taxes; it is equal to *gross income less expenses, outgoings, and taxation.

nett interest, the interest from an investment after taxation has been deducted from the *gross interest.

nett national product, the *gross national product excluding capital consumption.

nett price, the price of an article after deduction of any discounts, allowance, etc.

nett profit, 1. the *gross profit of a business less expenses and overheads. This is the profit shown on a *profit and loss account. **2.** the gross profit of a business less expenses, overheads, and taxation.

non-contributory pensions

nett tonnage, a measurement of the cargo-carrying capacity of a ship equal to the *gross tonnage less certain non-cargo spaces. *Also called* nett register tonnage.

nett weight, the weight of the goods in a container or vehicle excluding packaging material or the weight of the vehicle itself. It is equal to the *gross weight less the *tare.

nett worth, the value of the assets of a company after deduction of all liabilities.

nett yield, the *yield from an investment after deduction of taxation.

new issue, any shares or loan stock in a company or any government stock that has been offered for sale to the public for the first time.

night safe, a safe set into the outside wall of a bank to enable customers to deposit money in the bank outside working hours.

night shift, the night hours during which a factory, hospital, etc., is manned by workers. Factories involved in a continuous manufacturing process usually divide the day into three 8-hour shifts; the night shift is the last of these.

no-claims bonus, a discount given on the premium payable for a motor-car insurance policy, if the policyholder has not made a claim during the previous year.

nominal account, a book-keeping term for a ledger account that deals with revenue and expenditure other than creditors and debtors.

nominal capital, the total of the *nominal value of all the shares in a company.

nominal damages, a very small sum awarded as compensation by a court in a civil action, because the court decided that the person who brought the action, althought right, suffered no real loss.

nominal income, the wages or salary paid to a person excluding fringe benefits and overtime pay.

nominal ledger, a ledger containing, in summary form, the various accounts kept by a company. It enables the company to produce quickly the figures for a profit and loss account.

nominal partner, a partner who lends his name to an enterprise or company although he does not contribute work or capital to the partnership.

nominal price, an estimated price of an article. It may have to be estimated because the real value has not been established (by offering it for sale) or because there is no immediate market for it.

nominal value (par value), the face value of a security rather than its market value. For example a share issued at £1 may command a much greater price in the market.

nominal yield, the annual dividends received from a *security expressed as a percentage of its *nominal value.

nominee, a person named by another to act for him in some capacity.

nominee shareholding, shares bought by one person in the name of another person, bank, stockbroker, etc., in order to conceal the identity of the purchaser.

nonacceptance, the nonpayment of a *bill of exchange by the person on whom it is drawn.

non-assented stock, stock held by a person who, during the course of a *take-over bid, does not agree to accept the terms offered.

non-contributory pensions, a pension scheme in which all the contributions are made by the employers

75

nonfulfilment

for the employees' benefit, with no contributions from the employees.

nonfulfilment, failure to carry out a promise or contract.

nonprofitmaking concern, any organization set up for some purpose other than that of making a profit. Typical nonprofitmaking concerns are charities, hospitals, etc.

nontaxable income, income that is not liable to income tax. For example, personal allowances, interest on certain government stocks, unemployment or sickness benefits, etc.

nonvoting shares (A shares), shares in a company issued to raise capital although they do not give the holders the right to vote at company meetings. In other respects they usually confer equal rights to *ordinary shares.

nostro account, a bank account conducted by a U.K. bank with a bank in a foreign country. *Compare* vostro account.

notary public, a lawyer or solicitor empowered to attest documents, affidavits, etc.

notice of abandonment. *See* constructive total loss.

notice of motion, a formal notification sent to those about to attend a meeting, stating that a particular proposal will be made and discussed, following which the members of the meeting will be required to vote for or against the proposal.

noting, a procedure adopted if a *bill of exchange is dishonoured. The bill is handed to a *notary public with instructions to represent the bill; if it is still dishonoured the notary makes a note of the fact on the bill and in his register. This is a preliminary to a *protest.

notional income, a theoretical benefit that an owner receives from an asset. In some countries notional income is taxed, although it is usually difficult to assess.

not negotiable, words written on a *bill of exchange or a *cheque to make them non-negotiable. They can only be exchanged for money by the person to whom they are made out.

null and void, having no legal force or effect.

numbered account, a bank deposit account identified by a number to preserve the anonymity of the depositor. Swiss banks are usually only willing to provide this service for large deposits.

O

obsolescence, the process of becoming out of date. This process leads to a depreciation in the value of some capital goods, such as machines, cars, etc.

occupational hazard, a risk to health inherent in a particular type of work. For example, workers in certain chemical factories may develop skin diseases.

occupational mobility, the extent to which workers are willing to change their occupations and move to a different area.

O.C.R. *See* optical character recognition.

offer, a declaration by a seller that he is willing to sell certain specified goods for a specific price on specified terms. *See also* bid, counteroffer.

offer by prospectus, an offer of a *new issue of shares made directly by a company to the general public. The company provides the public with information in the form of a prospectus.

offer for sale, an offer of a *new issue of shares made by a company to the general public through the intermediary of a bank or similar institution. The bank purchases the whole new issue and then sells the shares to the public at a slightly higher price.

offer to purchase, a *takeover bid by a company for the shares of another company.

office hours, the hours of the day during which an office is open for business.

office manager, the person in charge of the clerks, book-keepers, etc., in an office.

official rate, the rate of exchange of a currency declared to be in force by the government or other agency controlling the currency. In making such a rate the government must be willing to defend the official rate on the foreign-exchange markets.

official receiver, a public official appointed by a government to arrange the *winding-up of the affairs of a bankrupt or of a bankrupt company. *See also* liquidator, trustee.

official strike, a *strike approved by a trade union as opposed to an *unofficial strike* that does not have union approval.

old-age pension, a pension paid by a government or an employer to a person when he reaches a certain age.

oligopoly, an industry in which there are many buyers but only a few sellers.

on approval, an arrangement that allows a customer to take goods home for a specified period in order to decide whether or not he wishes to purchase them.

on consignment, a type of export business in which goods are placed in the hands of an overseas agent with instructions to sell them at a specified price or at the market price. The seller does not receive payment until the goods are sold and the agent usually works for a commission.

on costs. *See* indirect costs.

on demand, *bills of exchange or

uncrossed cheques are payable on demand if the person to whom they are addressed will pay the sum specified when the bill is presented to them.

OPEC. *See* Organization of Petroleum Exporting Countries.

open cheque, an uncrossed cheque that is payable *on demand.

open cover, a form of marine insurance that covers all cargoes shipped during a specified period, usually one year. Declarations of shipments are made at the end of each week or month and premiums are calculated accordingly.

open credit, an arrangement that enables a customer of a bank to cash cheques at other specified branches of the bank.

open economy, the economy of a country in which foreign trading is important. *Compare* closed economy.

open general licence, a licence granted to an importer allowing him to import goods on which there are no specific restrictions.

open indent. *See* closed indent.

open-plan office, an office in which individuals do not have separate rooms but work in a large open area. This makes communication easier but is unpopular with those who value privacy.

open position, the position of a speculator who has purchased shares or commodities without *hedging.

open shop, a place of employment in which membership of a trade union is not a necessary requirement. *Compare* closed shop.

operating budget, a forecast of the running expenses of a company for a year, excluding capital expenditure. *Compare* capital budget.

operational research (OR), the investigation and analysis of particular activities in a company to determine the most efficient and economical way of carrying them out.

operator, 1. a person who works a machine. 2. a dealer or trader, especially one who takes a speculative position.

optical character recognition (O.C.R.), a method of introducing information into a computer. Text to be introduced is typed, using specially designed typefaces, and scanned by an optical character reader, which is a photoelectric device for converting images of letters into electrical signals.

option, a form of speculation enabling a person to purchase the right to buy or sell a specified amount of shares or commodities at a specified price at any time during a specified period. For this right he pays a sum called *option money*, which is forfeited if he does not take up his option to buy or sell. An option to sell is called a *put option and to buy a *call option; a *double option entitles the speculator either to buy or to sell.

option dealer, a dealer or broker who sells *options.

O.R. *See* operational research.

oral evidence, evidence given in court by word of mouth rather than in writing.

order, 1. a declaration by a person or company that he wishes to purchase specified goods or services. 2. an instruction issued by a court detailing the actions that must be taken by a person as a result of a judgment.

order book, a book containing a record of the orders taken by a company.

order cheque, a cheque that requires the *endorsement of the payee unless he pays it into his own banking account. Cheques are made payable to a specified person "or order". The person concerned may then transfer the cheque to another person by endorsing it on the back.

ordinary life assurance, *life assurance not having the special provisions and characteristics of *industrial life assurance designed to cater for lowly paid workers.

ordinary resolution, a resolution passed at a meeting of shareholders of a company by a majority of more than 50% of those present who are entitled to vote.

ordinary share, shares in a company that carry a right to vote at company meetings but do not carry a right to a *dividend. Dividends are paid only if the company has made a profit and if the directors have recommended that some or all of this profit should be distributed to shareholders.

organization and methods (O & M), a management technique involving the investigation and analysis of the efficiency of working methods in a company. For example, the design of a machine-tool, if improved, could lead to greater output on the part of its operator.

Organization of Petroleum Exporting Countries (OPEC), a consortium of oil-producing states whose objective is to regulate the prices of crude oil.

organized market, an established market, such as a stock exchange or a commodity exchange, that is recognized as a centre for dealing and where information regarding market movements can conveniently be exchanged.

origin, the country in which an imported product originated.

out of bond, goods released from a bonded warehouse after customs duties have been paid.

outstanding accounts, accounts that have not yet been settled.

outturn, the amount of revenue raised by taxation during a financial year rather than the figure estimated in the budget.

outworking, work carried out by the employees of a company in their own homes, using materials provided by the employers. This is quite a common practice in the clothing industry.

overcapitalization, a situation in which a company's nett *assets are less than its issued capital.

overdraft, the facility granted to a customer by a bank permitting him to draw out more money that he has in his current account. Interest is payable and is calculated on a daily basis, according to the amount of the debit balance. *Compare* bank loan.

overheads. *See* indirect costs.

over investment, excessive investment by a company in plant, machinery, etc., leading to surplus capacity when *demand falls.

overproduction, production in excess of *demand.

overseas agent. *See* agent.

overseas income taxation, income received from overseas that has been or will be taxed in the country of origin and will also be taxed by the country in which the recipient of the income is domiciled. Many countries have double-taxation agreements between themselves allowing a recipient of overseas income to obtain a rebate of tax in his own country.

oversubscribed issue. *See* application and allotment.

overtime, the hours worked by an employee that exceed the standard

overtrading

number of hours for which he is normally paid. Overtime hours are usually paid for at a higher rate than the basic rate.

overtrading, a situation in which a company's working capital is inadequate to cover the amount of business it has contracted to do. In such cases *cash-flow problems inevitably arise.

ownership, the legal right of possession of property, shares, etc.

P

package deal, an arrangement between parties in which all outstanding issues between them are settled together in one agreement.

packaging, the use of containers, wrappers, etc., both as a means of packing small quantities of goods for the consumer market and to stimulate sales by attractive design.

paid-up capital, the total sum of money paid by the shareholders of a company for fully paid shares.

paid-up policy, a life assurance policy that by agreement between the assured and the assurance company is paid out at a reduced rate because the assured ceases to pay further premiums.

paid-up share, a share that has been paid for in full at the face value.

pallet, a wooden frame used to support goods stored in warehouses. They are designed so that they can be lifted by fork-lift trucks, enabling the goods to be transported from one place to another without being removed from the pallet.

palletization, the use of *pallets in the storage and transport of goods.

paper money, 1. money in the form of banknotes. 2. banknotes, cheques, and *bills of exchange.

paper profit (or loss), the profit that theoretically accrues when the market value of an asset rises, although the asset has not been offered for sale. The profit is only realized when the asset is sold. *See* realized profit.

parcel, 1. a package of a size suitable to be sent through the post. 2. a quantity of goods offered for sale.

parcel ticket, a receipt issued by some shipping lines, in place of a *bill of lading, for small parcels.

parent company, a company that owns and controls several subsidiary companies.

pari passu, (Latin: simultaneously and equally) ranking equally. In commerce the expression is used of different classes of shares that are of equal entitlement in respect of dividends or capital repayment.

partial loss, (in marine insurance) an *average. *See also* particular average, general average.

participating preference shares, *preference shares that receive an additional share of the profits of a company after the ordinary shares have been allotted a specified dividend.

particular average, partial loss or damage to a ship or its cargo, when the loss affects only one shipowner or cargo owner. *See also* general average, free of particular average.

partly paid shares, shares that have been issued but for which the full nominal value has not been demanded, only a proportion having been paid.

partner, one of two or more people who own a business and share the profits in agreed proportions, as laid down in a *partnership agreement. *See also* general partner, limited partner, sleeping partner.

partnership, a form of business in which two or more people establish and run an enterprise as *partners. There are no shareholders, profits

partnership agreement

being shared between the partners. *See also* partnership agreement.

partnership agreement, the document laying down the terms upon which two or more *partners have entered into a business *partnership. The agreement will deal with share of profits, liabilities, capital invested, withdrawal of capital, etc.

part payment, a deposit paid by a buyer of goods, property, etc., to prove that he really intends to make the purchase.

par value, the denomination of a security (*see also* face value). The shares in a public company may have a denomination of £1, although their *issue price may be higher; neither the par value nor the issue price will dictate their market value after issue.

passing a name, the act of a broker in giving his principal the name of his client. When a broker passes a name he usually does not guarantee the solvency of the named client.

patent (*short for* letters patent), a sole right, granted by a government agency to an invention for a specified period (usually 16 years). For this right the inventor has to pay an annual fee. *See also* patent agent.

patent agent, a specialist in the preparation of applications for *patents. The agent has to show that his client's invention is sufficiently different from existing patented inventions in merit the grant of a new patent.

paternalism, a type of management that combines a benevolent interest in the welfare of its workforce with an implicit expectation of loyalty to the organization.

pawnbroker, a licensed moneylender who accepts goods as security. If loans are not repaid within a specified period the goods may be sold at public auction, the owner receiving the proceeds less the amount of the loan and the interest due.

payable at sight, words written on a *bill of exchange to indicate that it is payable on presentation to the *drawee.

payable on demand, words written on a *bill of exchange to indicate that it is payable by the *drawee on demand.

payable to bearer, words written on a *bill of exchange to indicate that it is not payable to a named person but to the bearer of the bill.

payable to order, words written on a *bill of exchange to indicate that there are no restrictions on its transfer by endorsement to a person other than the person named on the bill.

pay-as-you-earn (P.A.Y.E.), a tax-collecting system in which a person's income-tax is deducted by his employer before his salary is paid to him. The employer is responsible for remitting tax deducted to the taxation authorities.

payback period, the time that has to elapse before the nett income from an investment or commercial project is sufficient to repay the intial sum invested in it.

pay day, the day on which wages and salaries are paid.

P.A.Y.E. *See* pay-as-you-earn.

payee, 1. the person in whose favour a *bill of exchange or cheque is drawn. 2. any person to whom money is paid.

paying banker, the banker on whom a cheque or *bill of exchange is drawn.

paying-in book, a book issued by a bank to a customer to enable him to record payments made into his account.

payment by results, a method of paying workers by measuring the actual amount of work done. The most usual method is to pay *piece rates.

payment in advance, a payment made by a buyer before goods have been delivered or before a service has been rendered.

payment in due course, payment of a *bill of exchange on maturity.

payment in full, the settlement of a debt or account in full, i.e. the complete discharge of the debt.

payment in kind, payment in goods or services rather than in cash.

payment on account, a part payment of a debt.

payment stopped, an instruction by a drawer of a cheque to his bank to stop the payment of the cheque.

payment terms, the conditions agreed between parties for the payment of goods or services. The payment terms control the extent to which credit is given to the buyer by the seller.

pay pause, a government measure aimed at discouraging pay rises as part of a *prices and incomes policy.

payroll, 1. a list of the workers in a company showing the amount of wages due to each of them. **2.** the number of people employed by a firm.

payroll tax, a tax levied on the total of a company's *pay roll.

pay slip, a statement of wages or salary due to an employee given to him by his employer each pay day, showing the total amount of pay due less deductions for income tax (*see* pay-as-you-earn), insurance contributions, etc.

peak hours, those hours of the day when certain activities are at their maximum. For example, the peak hours for railways carrying workers to work centres are in the early morning when workers are going to work and in the late afternoon when they are returning home.

pegging the exchanges, government action to stabilize the value of its currency by fixing a value to it and supporting this value in the foreign-exchange markets.

penalty clause, a clause in a *contract providing for a specified amount of compensation to be paid by one party to the other should he fail to fulfil the terms of the contract.

pension, a regular payment made to a person who has retired in consideration of his past services. Pensions are usually related to the person's earnings when he leaves the company.

pensionable earnings, the basic earnings of an employer that are taken into account when calculating his *pension on retirement.

pensioner, a person who has retired on a *pension.

peppercorn rent, a nominal rent paid for a leasehold property.

P/E ratio. *See* price/earnings ratio.

per capita income, the ratio of the total income of all the people in a group to the number of people in the group. It is a measure of the average income of members of the group.

per contra, denoting a book-keeping entry made in an account to compensate for another entry wrongly made. For example, if the wrong account is debited with a sum it must be credited with the same sum per contra to keep the account in order.

peril, a risk, such as a storm or fire, especially one that can be covered by insurance.

period bill, a *bill of exchange payable

period of grace

on a specified date rather than on demand.

period of grace, the period allowed for payment of a *bill of exchange, usually three days unless the bill is payable *at sight or *on demand.

perishable goods, goods, such as food, that only remain saleable for a limited period.

permit, a document giving the bearer permission to do something that is specified.

perpetual debenture, a *debenture that cannot be redeemed on demand.

perpetual inventory, an *inventory of the stock of materials on which day-to-day changes are entered.

perpetual succession, the continuance of a company until it is wound-up or liquidated. As a company is, in law, a separate entity its continuation is independent of the survival of its owners or directors.

per pro, (Latin: per procurationem) an abbreviation, often further shortened to p.p., to indicate that a person is signing a document on behalf of another. Such as a person should hold a *power of attorney to do so but in practice rarely does.

personal accident and sickness insurance, an insurance policy providing for compensation in the case of accidents causing death or injury or for disablement through disease or sickness incurred through specified causes.

personal account, an account in a ledger that records transactions with a specified debtor or creditor.

personal assistant, an assistant to a business executive.

personal loan, a loan made by a bank to a customer to cover some item of personal expenditure. Interest is charged and is usually paid monthly together with loan repayment instalments.

personal wealth, the value of an individual's personal possessions including property, money, shares, insurance policies, etc.

personnel, the workforce or staff employed by a business.

personnel management, the part of the management of a business organization that is concerned with selecting, recruiting, and training employees.

personnel selection, the process of recruiting staff for a business organization by means of interviews and suitable tests.

persuasive advertising, the form of *advertising that emphasizes the distinctive characteristics of a product rather than offering prospective buyers information about it. Compare informative advertising.

petrodollars, dollars accumulated by the oil-producing countries, that are in excess of those countries' needs and are invested in developed countries.

petty cash, a relatively small amount of money kept on business premises to meet small incidental expenses.

picket, a guard or guards belonging to a trade union, who prevent workers from entering their place of work during a strike.

piece rate, a form of *payment by results in which wages are paid at a specified rate for work carried out and not on the basis of time spent doing the work.

pie chart, a diagram consisting of a circle with a number of radii forming sectors (like slices of a pie), each of which repesents a specific proportion of the whole. It is used to illustrate the proportions into which something is divided.

pilot plant, a small-scale production plant for a new product, used in

post script

*pilot production to test manufacturing methods.

pilot production, production of a new product on a small scale to test methods of production and the marketability of the product.

placing, a method of selling a *new issue of shares in which a stockbroker disposes of the shares to his clients without need for a market quotation.

planned economy, an economy is which the allocation of resources is planned and controlled by the government, rather than being left to the laws of supply and demand.

planned location of industry, encouragement given by a government to industry to set up factories in areas of high unemployment, by means of subsidies, tax concessions, etc.

planning blight, a fall in the value of a property, area, etc., resulting from the publication of a government development plan that affects the district.

pledge, 1. something given as a security. 2. a promise.

Plimsoll line, another name for *load line.

ploughed-back profits, the part of the annual profits of a company remaining after dividends have been paid that is set aside to finance the growth of the company.

pluvial insurance, insurance against losses incurred by bad weather, especially heavy rain.

point of sale, a shop or other place in which goods are retailed to the public.

policy. See insurance policy.

policy proof of interest (P.P.I.), the right of the holder of an insurance policy to receive payment of any claims. Possession of the policy is important as the possessor may have lent money to the policyholder and taken the policy as security.

poll tax, an outright tax levied on every person defined as being liable to pay it, irrespective of their income or circumstances.

population projection, a forecast of the size of a population in the future. It is necessary to make such forecasts for planning purposes.

population pyramid, a diagram illustrating the ditribution by age of a population. The older age groups from the top of the pyramid with the younger, and more numerous, people forming the base.

portfolio, a record of the investments of an individual or an institution.

portmark, one of the marks stencilled onto a package (bag, drum, crate, etc.) for shipment by sea or air. It states the port of destination.

port of call, a port at which ships call to take on fuel or stores, to load or unload cargo or passengers, etc.

port of destination, the port to which exported goods are shipped for delivery to the overseas buyers.

postal order, a money order bought from a post office for transmission to a person who is able to cash it at his local post office.

postcode, letters and numbers forming part of an address to assist in the sorting and delivery of mail.

post-dated, dated in advance. For example, a post-dated cheque may be issued by a person because he currently does not have funds to meet it.

poste restante, an international arrangement enabling travellers to have their mail delivered to a post office at their intended destinations for collection on arrival. In the U.S. this service is called *general delivery.*

post script, a note added as an afterthought to a letter, prefaced by the letters P.S.

power of attorney, a deed legally authorizing one person to act for another, as stipulated in the document.

P.P. *See* per pro.

pratique, a licence issued by port authorities to a ship giving it a clean bill of health after a period of quarantine.

preference share, a fixed-interest security that carries a prior claim over ordinary shareholders in the distribution of profits. This means that the division of profits to ordinary shareholders can only be made after the preferential shareholders have been paid.

preferential creditor, a *creditor who is entitled to be paid what is due to him before the claims of other creditors are met.

preferential duty, a reduced import duty favouring one particular country or group of countries for a particular type of product.

preliminary expenses, the expenses, such as registration and advertising, involved in forming a company.

premium, 1. a regular payment made to an insurance company by a policy holder. **2.** a sum paid in addition to the price of something in order to secure an additional advantage, such as early delivery. **3.** the amount by which a security stands above its *par value.

premium bonus, an additional payment made to a worker who has completed a task in a shorter time than allotted.

premium offer, a sales promotion in which the public are offered various goods at reduced prices in exchange for packet tops, labels, etc., taken from the product being promoted.

prepayment, a payment that is made before goods or services have been received.

present value, a method of assessing the current nett value of future benefits and outlays in a business venture. It enables the investor to determine whether or not an enterprise is going to be worthwhile, from the profit point of view, compared with simply lending the capital at interest.

president, the managing director of a U.S. company.

pre-tax profit, the trading profit of a business after deduction of expenses and overheads but before deductions of taxation. *See* gross profit.

price, the cost of something or the cost per unit.

price control, the control of retail prices by a government to safeguard an economy against inflation.

price discrimination, charging different prices for goods or services to different markets, according to what each market will bear.

price/earnings ratio, the ratio of the market price of a share to the earnings per share. The ratio is used by market analysts as an indication of the value of a company as an investment, usually compared to other companies in the same industry.

price leader, a company that controls a substantial portion of a market for a particular product and is therefore in a position to set the price for that product in the knowledge that competitors will set their prices at a similar level to avoid a *price war.

price ring, a *cartel on a small scale in which a number of companies or dealers agree to fix minimum prices for their products or services.

prices and incomes policy, a government policy, particularly in a period

produce

of inflation, that aims to keep wages or salaries from rising too quickly by means of *price controls.

price support, the subsidizing of certain products by a government by fixing minimum prices for the products above the market level. The object is to maintain the level of incomes of the producers.

price war, competition between companies producing similar goods in which each attempts to undercut the others' prices in order to capture a larger share of the market.

prime costs. *See* direct costs.

prime entry books, books of account kept by a company, recording details of purchases and sales on a day-to-day basis. Entries are transformed from these books to the *ledgers.

prime rate, the basic rate of interest charged by commercial banks in the U.S. This rate would normally be charged only to customers with the very highest creditworthiness, others being charged at higher rates.

principal, 1. the capital sum of money upon which interest is earned. **2.** a person or company on whose behalf an agent acts.

prior charges, the dividends, interest, or capital repayment paid to *debenture shareholders or *preference shareholders, before distributions to *ordinary shareholders.

private carrier. *See* carrier.

private company, a company that may not offer its shares to the general public. In the U.K., membership of such a company is limited to 50, excluding employees. *Compare* public company.

private costs, costs involved in the conduct of a business, a company, or individual. *Compare* social costs.

private enterprise, an economic system in which members of the public transact business on their own account for profit.

private health insurance, insurance to provide cover for a person requiring private medical treatment with a doctor of his own choice as opposed to treatment under a government health scheme.

private limited company, a *private company in which the liability of directors is limited. *See* limited company.

private placing, the taking up of the whole of a new issue of shares by a financial institution, such as an issuing house. The shares are later sold in blocks to large investors, such as insurance companies.

private sector, the part of the economy of a country that works by *private enterprise and is not under government ownership, though it may be subjected to some government restrictions.

private treaty, a deal arranged privately between buyer and seller, rather than by public auction or on the open market.

probability, a mathematical expression of the likelihood that some event will occur. If it is certain not to happen the probability that it will happen is 0, while if it is certain to happen it will have a probability of 1.

probate, the process of proving that a will is valid.

procuration, a *power of attorney given by one person to another. The person who holds this power signs documents on behalf of his principal putting *per pro or p.p. before his name.

produce, commercial commodities, such as rubber, jute, grain, wool, groundnuts, etc., that are produced agriculturally.

produce brokers

produce brokers, a *commodity broker who specializes in the *produce markets.

produce market, a market in which *produce is traded, especially for future delivery (see futures market).

product, any manufactured article of trade.

production, the conversion of raw materials into consumable articles. In the strict economic sense it also includes the provision of services of value to consumers.

production control, coordination of the many operations in a manufacturing industry to achieve the efficient and economical production of goods of the required quality.

production engineering, the branch of engineering concerned with the construction and control of industrial production processes.

productive labour, the part of a community's workforce that produces goods, as opposed to the workforce producing services.

productivity, the output of an industry in relation to the input in terms of labour, materials, or cost.

products guarantee insurance, an insurance against claims arising from the failure of a product to work as it should. The cover provides for the repair or replacement of the product.

products liability insurance, an insurance policy covering a producer, supplier, or repairer against his legal liability should a *product cause loss, damage, or injury to the purchaser.

professional indemnity insurance, an insurance policy covering a professional person, such as an accountant or a solicitor, against his legal liability should his negligence cause loss, damage, or injury to a client.

professional valuation, an assessment of the value of the assets of a company by a qualified person.

profit, monetary gain resulting from the investment of capital or labour in some enterprise or transaction.

profitability, a measure of the relative merits of two or more projects, products, businesses, etc., from the point of view of their ability to make a profit.

profit and loss account, an annual statement summarizing a company's revenue and costs and therefore its profit or loss.

profiteer, a person who seeks to make an excessive profit by taking advantage of shortages of goods, especially in time of war or disaster.

profit motive, the motive that makes people start and run businesses in a *private enterprise economy or in the private sector of a mixed economy.

profit-sharing, the distribution of some of the profits of a business to employees to encourage them to take an interest in the profitability of the business.

profits tax, a tax levied on the profits of a company.

profit-taking, selling securities, commodities, etc., after a rise in price in order to be certain of making a profit.

pro-forma invoice, a provisional invoice sent to a purchaser before the goods have been sent to him or before the exact weights have been agreed.

progress chaser, a person in a factory whose job is to ensure that production is going according to plan, without bottlenecks or breakdowns in the chain of processes.

progressive tax, an *income tax that becomes proportionately larger as income becomes higher.

public liability insurance

prohibitive tariff, a tariff introduced with the object of preventing a commodity from being imported into a country. The tariff is set so high that the price of the commodity affected would become unsaleable.

promissory note, a note from one person to another, promising to pay him a specified sum of money on a certain date.

promoter, a person concerned in the formation of a company.

promotion, 1. the launching of a new company. **2.** any method of increasing the sales of a product, especially one using advertising. **3.** an advance from one rank or status in a job to a higher one.

prompt cash, payment terms for goods purchased that demand settlement immediately on delivery, or within a few days of delivery.

prompt day, the day on which payment is due for a purchase of goods.

prompt delivery, delivery terms for goods purchased that call for the goods to be delivered from seller to buyer immediately.

property, 1. anything owned by a person. **2.** formerly a distinction was made between *real property* (freehold land) and *personal property* (leasehold land and other possessions).

property bonds, bonds offered by *unit trusts in which the funds raised are invested in properties or property shares.

property insurance, an insurance against loss of, or damage to, property.

property tax, a tax on land and buildings.

proprietary company (Pty), a private limited company registered in South Africa or Australia.

pro rata, in proportion.

prospectus, detailed information regarding a company, published when the company offers its shares for purchase by the general public.

protective duty, a customs duty levied on imports to protect the home producers of similar products.

protest, a certificate, signed by a *notary public, stating that payment or acceptance of a *bill of exchange has been refused.

proximo, of next month. Often abbreviated to *prox*. E.g. 24th prox. refers to the 24th of next month. *Compare* instant, ultimo.

proxy, a person who acts for another.

Pty. *See* proprietary company.

public company, a company whose shares can be purchased by the general public, usually through a *stock exchange. *Compare* private company.

public corporation, an organization that is appointed by a government to run a nationalized industry.

public debts, the debts of state-owned institutions, including those of local authorities, etc.

public deposits, the money held by a government. In the U.K. it is held by the Bank of England on behalf of the government.

public enterprise, an organization that provides a public service, such as a water-supply company or a nationalized industry, and is owned by the government although it could function as a *private enterprise.

public good, something that is beneficial to a community but has no easily assessable financial value.

public issue, an *issue of shares offered for sale to the public.

public liability insurance, insurance against risks involving death, injury,

public ownership

disease, or damage to members of the public.

public ownership, the possession by the state of industries, public service organizations, etc.

public relations, the promotion and maintenance of goodwill between an organization and the public generally.

public sector, that part of the economy that is under *public ownership. For example, hospitals, schools, and the nationalized industries. *Compare* private sector.

public trustee, an official of the government whose services are available to the public to act in *trust matters.

public warehouse, a warehouse at or near a port for storing goods awaiting shipment or goods that have recently arrived.

public works, buildings, roads, bridges, etc., constructed and owned by the state.

punter, a speculator, especially one who attempts to make quick profits on a *stock exchange or *commodity market.

purchase journal, a book of account in which the purchases of a business are recorded on a daily basis.

purchase ledger, a book of account that records all the purchases made by a business. It is usually arranged alphabetically under the names of the suppliers and shows payments made and amounts outstanding.

purchase tax, a tax levied on goods at the point of sale.

purchasing officer, an official of an organization authorized to buy raw materials, etc.

purchasing power, the ability of a unit of money to buy goods or services. In times of *inflation, when the prices of goods are rising, the purchasing power of the currency declines.

purser, a ship's officer who is responsible for keeping accounts, looking after the needs of passengers, etc.

put option, an *option to sell shares, commodities, etc., at their current price within a specified period. To buy such an option costs a specified sum of money, which is forfeited if the option is not taken up. Thus, if the price of the share or commodity falls by more than the cost of buying the option, the buyer will exercise his option to sell the shares or commodity and be able to buy them back more cheaply and so make a profit. *Compare* call option.

pyramid selling, a method of selling goods, securities, etc., using part-time salesmen. The seller recruits a team of area managers who buy a right to sell the goods and usually a quantity of the goods themselves. The area managers recruit a number of distributors, each of whom buy a portion of the goods. These distributors again sub-divide their holdings, selling to door-to-door salesmen, who sell direct to the public. The method is controlled in some countries to prevent the distribution network becoming so large that the market for the goods is swamped, leaving members of the network with unsaleable goods.

Q, R

qualified acceptance, the acceptance of a *bill of exchange that varies the effect of the bill as drawn. For example, it may be accepted payable at only one place or accepted by some but not all of the drawers.

quality control, systematic checks of a percentage of the products coming off a production line to ensure that the quality of the product meets the required specification.

quantity rebate, a *discount given for buying in bulk.

quantity surveyor, a specialist in the building and construction industry who gives estimates of the quantities of materials required for a project and their probable costs.

quantum meruit, (Latin: as much as he has earned), the basis of a claim for partial payment for work done or goods supplied, although a *contract may not have been completed.

quarter days, the four days marking the quarters of the year: 25th March (Lady Day), 24th June (Midsummer Day), 29th September (Michaelmas), and 25th December (Christmas Day). On these days certain payments, such as rents, fall due.

quick assets, *assets that can quickly be converted into cash.

quid pro quo, (Latin: something for something) something that must be given in exchange for something that has been received.

quorum, the minimum number of members (or their representatives) of an organization that must be present at a meeting in order to make decisions taken at the meeting binding on all the members.

quotation, 1. an *offer that is not firm. 2. the current price of a share listed on a *stock exchange.

quoted company, a company whose shares are quoted on a *stock exchange.

quoted price, 1. the official price of a commodity, as quoted by the market dealing in that commodity. 2. the price of a security as quoted in the official records of a *stock exchange.

rally, a recovery in the market price of a security or commodity after a previous fall in price.

random sample, a sample taken in such a way that all the items to be sampled have an equal (or known) chance of being selected.

rate of exchange, the current price of one currency in relation to another.

rate of interest. *See* interest rate.

rate rebate, a discount deducted from the local *rates. It may be applicable to all ratepayers or to a restricted number of ratepayers, such as old-age pensioners.

rates, a tax levied on local residents by local authorities to pay for certain amenities. The tax is determined by the rateable value of the residence, as fixed by a valuation officer.

ratify, to confirm or approve.

rationalization, a reorganization of resources, etc., for the sake of efficiency or economy. For example, a company with a refinery in one area could agree with another company with a refinery in another area that each should satisfy their customers' requirements in their own areas.

raw material

raw material, material, such as wool or crude oil, that is used in a manufacturing process, before it has been processed.

real estate, land, buildings, or property that is immoveable.

realization account, the final *profit and loss account of a company that has been wound-up or liquidated.

realize, to convert into cash.

realized profit, a capital gain that has been converted into cash. *Compare* paper profit.

real property. *See* property.

realtor, the U.S. name for an estate agent.

real value, the value of an asset in terms that takes into account any changes in the value of money. For example, an asset valued at £100 in one year may be worth £200 five years later. But if the price index for that kind of asset has also doubled in the period, its real value will not have altered.

real wages, the current value of wages in terms of purchasing power. If prices are rising more rapidly than *money wages, real wages will be falling.

rebate, a discount.

receipt, an acknowledgement in writing that a payment for something has been made.

received for shipment, words added to a *bill of lading signifying that the goods are alongside the ship and awaiting loading. *Compare* shipped bill.

receiver, a person appointed to supervise the winding up of a person's or a company's affairs. *See also* official receiver.

receiving order, an order issued by a court putting the *official receiver in charge of the affairs of an insolvent person or company in order to advise the court whether or not the debtor should be declared *bankrupt.

recession, a period during which trade is declining, production and investment is falling, and unemployment is rising.

reciprocity, any agreement between two parties in which one makes concessions to the other in order to achieve the terms he wants. For example, one country may agree to reduce its import duty on one range of goods, provided that the other country reduces its tariff on another range of goods.

recognizance, an agreement between a person and a court of law binding that person to carry out a particular act, such as a promise to appear in court on a certain date.

recommended retail selling price, the published price of an article as recommended by the manufacturer. The retailer may sell below this price if he wishes to do so.

recorded delivery, a U.K. postal service providing a record of posting and delivery of mail. Should loss or damage occur to such mail, the Post Office would be liable for compensation.

recourse agreement, an agreement between parties that in certain circumstances compensation shall become payable or some other action shall be taken. For example, when someone fails to keep up hire-purchase payments, the seller of the goods, by agreement with the hire-purchase company, will repossess the goods.

recovery, a period following a *depression during which trade is improving, production and investment is rising, and unemployment is falling.

redeemable security, any security

that is repayable on a specified date at *par or at a *redemption premium.

redemption, the ability of a security to be exchanged for cash on a specified date.

redemption date, the date upon which a *redeemable security is due for repayment.

redemption premium, the amount by which the price of a *redeemable security exceeds its *par value.

redemption yield, the annual return on a *fixed-interest security, taking into account any loss or gain in its capital value over the remainder of its life. For example, if a security with a market value of £90 per unit is redeemable at £100 in 5 years, its redemption yield will exceed its *current yield by $10/5 \div 100 = 2\%$.

redeployment of labour, the movement of labour from one industry to another, often as a result of government policy.

rediscount, to discount a *bill of exchange that has already been discounted.

redistribution of income, the use of *progressive taxation to reduce excessive inequalities of income, especially as a measure taken by a socialist government.

redundancy, 1. the loss of jobs when employees are no longer needed by their employers, either because of poor demand or as a result of an internal reorganization. **2.** the money paid to an employee when he is made redundant, either by his employer or by a government.

re-exports, goods imported into a country and exported to another country. *See also* entrepôt trade.

reference, 1. a written testimony as to the ability, character, honesty, etc., of a person. **2.** a person who is prepared to provide such a testimony.

refer to drawer, an endorsement made on a cheque that is not accepted by the bank upon which it is drawn, indicating that the drawer has insufficient funds in his account.

reflation, the relaxation of government controls upon a country's economy in order to increase demand, increase production, and lower unemployment.

refund, a repayment, often one made as a result of a complaint that goods delivered are not equal to the selling specification.

registered capital, the amount of capital for which a company may issue shares. In the U.K. it is the amount registered with the Registrar of Companies. *See also* authorized capital.

registered company, a company registered by the Registrar of Companies in the U.K.

registered land certificate, a certificate issued by the Land Registry in the U.K. to the owner of registered land.

registered name, the name of a company as registered with the Registrar of Companies in the U.K.

registered office, the official office or headquarters of a company to which official documents are delivered. It is registered with the Registrar of Companies in the U.K.

registered stock. *See* inscribed stock.

register of members, a register of the shareholders of a company.

reinsurance, a method of reducing an insurer's risk in which he covers a part of a policy with another insurance company or underwriter. For example, the insurance claim on a jumbo jet might be too large for one insurer if it became a total

remuneration

loss. He would therefore cover part of the risk with other insurers.

remuneration, the money paid to a person in return for his services.

rendu. *See* franco.

renewal notice, a notification by an insurance company that a premium is due on a policy and should be paid by a stipulated date or the policy will lapse.

rent, a payment made to an owner for the use of land, buildings, equipment, etc.

rent control, control by a government of the rent that a property owner can legally charge for leasing the property.

rent freeze, the fixing of rents, by government order, at their existing levels for a specified period, usually as a counter-inflationary measure.

rentier, a person whose income is derived from an asset rather than a salary.

renting back, a method of raising capital in which a person or company sells property, such as a house or factory, to a financial organization, such as a bank or insurance company, on the understanding that the organization will lease the property back to the seller.

renunciation, a declaration by a shareholder that he does not wish to take up the shares allocated to him in a *rights issue. The declaration may or may not state in whose favour the renunciation is made.

reparations, compensation for damage or injury caused, particularly by a defeated nation following a war.

repatriation, 1. the act of sending a person back to his own country. **2.** the transfer of capital from overseas to a person's own country.

replacement cost, the cost of replacing an asset, such as a machine tool, at current market prices.

reply-paid envelope, an envelope that is addressed to the sender and already stamped.

report of the directors, a report by the directors of a company that accompanies the periodic presentation of the company's accounts. It usually surveys trading in the past period and outlines prospects for the coming period.

representative, a commercial traveller employed by a company to sell its products. Sometimes shortened to "rep".

repudiation, a declaration by a party to a contract that he is not willing to fulfil its terms.

reputed owner, a person who, with the real owner's consent, appears to own a property.

requisitioning, the compulsory taking over of a property by a government without a change of ownership. The owner may or may not receive *rent. *Compare* compulsory purchase.

resale price maintenance, a marketing arrangement in which a retailer agrees to sell products at prices not lower than those suggested by the manufacturer.

reserve, the price below which a seller will not allow goods to be sold at a public auction. If the bidding for a lot does not reach the reserve the lot is withdrawn.

reserve currency, foreign currency, such as U.S. dollars, held by a country to finance international trade.

reserve for bad debts, an estimate of debts that are unlikely to be paid, which are shown in the accounts of a company so that tax need not be paid on them.

reserve for obsolescence, money set aside to replace an asset, such as a machine-tool, that has become obsolete before it has been fully depreciated.

rights issue

reserves, the portion of the profits that are not distributed to shareholders but are held for further investment or to enable the company to survive a bad period.

residual unemployment, the number of unemployed people who would be out of work even in times of full employment. They are usually unemployable for reasons of physical or mental handicap.

residuary legatee, the person who inherits what is left of an estate after all specific legacies and expenses have been paid.

resolution, a subject discussed at a formal meeting and passed as a decision to take some action.

restitution, 1. compensation for loss, damage, or injury. **2.** a court order for property to be returned to its rightful owner.

restraint of trade, any agreement between parties that restricts trade in a way that is against the interests of the public.

restrictive covenant, a provision in a contract that restricts one of the parties from taking a specified action.

restrictive endorsement, an endorsement on a *bill of exchange preventing the holder from negotiating it.

retailer, a person selling goods directly to the public.

retail price, the price of goods sold by a *retailer to the public.

retail price index. *See* cost-of-living index.

retained earnings, profits made by a business that are not distributed to the shareholders, but are retained as *reserves.

retention money, money held back by a buyer for work done pending his satisfaction that it has been properly carried out.

retirement pension, a pension paid to a person who has reached retirement age or who has retired for some other reason. It may be paid by an employer or by a government.

retiring a bill, the withdrawal of a *bill of exchange from circulation after it has been paid.

retroactive, denoting an order, statute, etc., that has effect from a specified date in the past.

return on capital, the ratio of profit earned by a business, investment, etc., to the capital employed in it.

revaluation, an increase in the value of a country's currency as a result of changing its exchange rate in terms of other currencies. *Compare* devaluation.

revenue, the income of a person, company, or state derived from all sources.

reverse takeover, the acquisition of a larger company by a smaller one.

reversionary annuity. *See* contingent annuity.

revocable letter of credit, a *letter of credit that can be cancelled by either the purchaser or the issuing bank. *Compare* irrevocable letter of credit.

revocation, the act of revoking or cancelling an agreement.

revolving credit, a credit with a bank that is renewed automatically when the amount is used up. There may be restrictions on the total amount of the credit or on the amount that can be used at any one time.

rigging a market, buying or selling in a market, with the object of making a profit, on a scale that could not be sustained for very long but that has the effect of raising or lowering prices to the speculator's advantage.

rights issue, an *issue of shares to existing shareholders entitling them to purchase a quantity of the new

rights letter

shares in direct proportion to their holdings.

rights letter, a letter informing a shareholder that the company is to make a *rights issue to existing shareholders on advantageous terms. If the shareholder does not wish to accept the offer he may sell the letter.

ring, an arrangement between dealers not to bid against one another at auctions, thus keeping prices low. After an auction, the dealers auction the goods acquired among themselves. This is an illegal practice.

riot and civil commotion, an insurable risk against the possibility that civil disorder will delay the implementation of a contract.

risk, the chance that an event will occur, especially one that has a known probability and that can be insured against.

risk capital, capital available for investment in a venture that does not quarantee a return and may involve a loss, although there is a possibility of a substantial capital gain.

river dues, fees payable by the owners of vessels for the use of rivers or inland waterways.

road haulage, the transport of goods by road vehicles.

rolling stock, railway carriages, trucks, etc.

rotation of directors, the rules of an organization often require a specified number of *directors to retire each year, although they may offer themselves for formal re-election at the *annual general meeting.

royalty, money paid for the right to use another person's property. For example a publisher pays an author a royalty on each of the author's books sold.

rummage, to search a ship for contraband goods.

running days, consecutive days, including Sundays. *Compare* working days.

run (on a bank), the withdrawal of funds from a bank by depositors who have lost confidence in the bank.

S

s.a.e. *See* stamped addressed envelope.

safe, a steel container for protecting money and other valuables against fire and theft.

safe custody, a service, sometimes provided by banks, for keeping documents, cash, and other valuables in their *strong rooms or vaults.

safe deposit, a place, such as the vault of a bank, in which documents and valuables can be stored, usually in a small individal safe.

sailing date, the date on which a ship is scheduled to leave a particular port for a particular destination.

salary, a fixed regular payment made to an employee. Salaries are usually paid at monthly intervals to clerical and managerial staff, whereas wages are paid weekly to manual workers.

sale, 1. a transaction in which the ownership of goods passes from one person or firm (the seller) to another (the buyer). **2.** an event in which a business, usually a shop, offers its surplus goods at reduced prices.

sale by auction, a method of selling goods or property in which an auctioneer (the seller or his representative) offers the goods in public, the sale being made to the highest bidder.

sale or return, a method of selling in which the seller, usually a manufacturer or wholesaler, agrees to take back from the buyer, usually a retailer, any goods that he is unable to sell.

sales agent, a person or firm appointed by a manufacturer to sell his products in a particular area.

sales force, all the salesmen employed by an organization.

sales ledger, a book in which all the sales made by a firm are recorded, together with the price, quantity, and quality of the goods and the date on which payment was received.

sales letter, a letter sent out by a firm, usually to a large number of possible clients, to advertise its products.

salesman, a person employed by a company to sell its products, either on its own premises or by travelling around the country (*travelling salesman*).

sales promotion, activities, such as demonstrations or price reductions, to increase the sales of a company's products.

sales resistance, unwillingness on the part of potential customers to buy a particular product or brand in spite of efforts to persuade them to do so.

sales tax, a tax paid by the purchaser of goods, such as petrol, at the time purchase is made. Sometimes the tax is concealed in the price.

salvage, money obtained by the sale of ships or cargoes that have been damaged by fire or shipwreck or by selling other goods that have been damaged by fire or accident. The sale is usually made by an insurance company to set against the cost of the claim.

sample, a small quantity of goods that represents in all respects a larger quantity. Samples are given to potential buyers to help them decide whether or not they wish to make a purchase.

sampling order, a document that authorizes the holder to take samples of goods held in a warehouse.

sandwich course, a form of study for technical qualifications, usually consisting of alternating periods of full-time study at a technical college and supervised practical experience in a factory or workshop.

sans recours, French for *without recourse.

savings, money that has been put aside for use in the future, often to provide for sickness or old age.

savings account, a form of bank account into which small regular payments are made to accumulate interest on the accumulated capital.

scale effect, a reduction in the average cost of producing a product as output is increased.

scarcity, a shortage of goods that occurs when the demand for them exceeds the supply.

schedule, 1. a detailed programme showing the timing of events, such as the sequence of processes in the manufacture of a particular product. **2.** a detailed list often attached to another document.

scheduled territories, the official name given to the *sterling area.

scrip issue, a free issue of shares given to existing shareholders of a company, usually in proportion to their holding.

seal, a circle of wax or paper having an impressed design to give authenticity to a document or to show that an envelope has not been opened.

seasonal fluctuation, a variation in the demand for a product that depends on the time of the year. For example, in temperate climates there is a seasonal variation in the demand for ice cream.

seasonal unemployment, a variation in the level of unemployment that depends on the time of the year. For example, there is more unemployment in the building trade during the winter months than at other times.

sea-water damage, damage to goods caused by sea-water, usually occurring during the course of shipping the goods from one place to another.

seaworthy, denoting a ship that is fit to make an ocean voyage.

secondary banking sector, a group of companies providing a less comprehensive range of banking facilities than *commercial banks. For example, secondary banks do not provide current-account facilities.

secondhand goods, goods offered for sale that have had one or more previous owners.

second mortgage, a mortgage taken out on a property that has already been mortgaged once in order to raise money. The sum of the two mortgages must not exceed the value of the property.

second of exchange, a copy of a *bill of exchange sent by a different route in case the original is lost.

secretary, an employee whose duties include typing correspondence, organizing and taking minutes at meetings, filing, etc. *See also* company secretary.

secret reserve. *See* hidden reserve.

secured creditor, a creditor whose claims against a bankrupt or debtor are paid before those of an *unsecured creditor.

secured debenture, a debenture that has one or more of the assets of a company as security if it is not repaid on the repayment date.

secured liability, a liability having as security sufficient assets to protect the creditor against loss.

security, 1. any commercial document, such as a share, bond, debenture, government stock, etc., that can be bought and sold. **2.** assets specified by the borrower as a guarantee for a loss.

self-employed, working for one's own benefit in a business or profession rather than for a company in return for a fixed salary.

self-service, denoting a shop, garage, restaurant, etc., in which the customers serve themselves.

sell, to provide a customer with goods or services in exchange for payment.

seller's market, a market in which demand exceeds supply with the effect that prices usually rise. *Compare* buyer's market.

sellers over, a description of a market in which there are still sellers after all the buyers have been satisfied.

selling cost, the cost incurred in the selling of a product; it includes advertising, special packages, free gifts, etc.

selling price, the price at which goods or services are for sale; it is decided by the direct cost plus a contribution to the seller's overheads and profit.

semiskilled, denoting a workman who falls between an unskilled labourer and a skilled craftsman.

sensitive market, a description of a market in which prices move significantly in response to outside events, rumours, etc.

sequestration, the confiscation of property by a third party until a dispute is settled.

service, an activity that satisfies a need but is not a tangible commodity. Examples are transport, education, legal advice, etc.

service charge, a charge made in restaurants and hotels instead of a *tip.

service contract, a document setting out the terms of a director's contract with his company.

service industry, the section of industry concerned with providing *services.

services, electricity, water, gas, drainage, etc., as supplied to industrial and residential buildings.

set off, to subtract a sum of money owed to another person from that person's debt so that the debt is reduced.

settlement, the completion of a business or legal transaction by making the necessary payments.

severable contract, a contract that can be split into parts by a court of law, so that each part can be treated separately.

severance payment, a sum of money paid to a director or other employee when he is required to leave the company.

share, one of the large number of parts into which the ownership of a company is divided. Shares in *public companies may be bought and sold on a stock exchange, whereas those in private companies are bought and sold privately.

share capital, the amount of money a company has raised or is authorized to raise by issuing shares.

share certificate, a document proving ownership of shares.

shareholder, a person or organization that owns one or more shares in a company.

share index, a number calculated regularly to show changes in share prices generally or in particular groups of shares with respect to the prices in the year taken as the base for the index.

share premium

share premium, an extra charge on a *new issue of shares when the profitability of the company makes them appear more valuable then their nominal value.

share register, a register kept by a limited company of its shareholders.

shares of no par value, shares having no face value. They may, however, have a market value.

share transfer, a document proving that a certain number of shares have been transferred from one owner to another.

shift, 1. one of two or more groups of workers doing similar work during different set periods of the day. 2. the period worked by each of these groups.

shiftwork, the type of employment that involves working different *shifts.

ship, to transport goods from one place to another by sea.

shipbroker, a *broker who sells cargo space and charters, on behalf of shipowners, to shippers.

shipment from origin, shipment of goods, such as commodities, from a port in the country in which they were produced.

shipment of goods, the transporting of goods from one country to another by sea. Shipment is by liner sailing on an advertised route, by tramp steamer sailing on a charter, or by tanker.

shipowner's lien, the right of a shipowner to confiscate a cargo if the freight on it has not been paid.

shipped bill, a *bill of lading showing that a particular consignment of goods has been loaded onto a ship.

shipper, a firm that exports goods by sea or by air; the shipper may not be the producer of the goods but he usually pays the freight.

shipping and forwarding agent, a company specializing in handling goods that are being imported or exported by sea or air. It deals with all related documents, insurance, customs, etc.

shipping bill, a document that has to be completed by a shipper of goods to obtain *drawback from the customs.

shipping clerk, a clerk responsible for preparing the necessary documents for the import and export of goods by sea or air.

shipping company, a company that owns or operates ships.

shipping line, a group of ships owned or operated by a company.

ship's certificate of registry, a document listing the name, tonnage, country of registration, master, and owner of a ship.

ship's chandler, a person or company that sells ship's stores and fittings.

ship's master, the captain of a merchant ship.

ship's option, a method of quoting general cargo freight rates according to weight or measurement, whichever is the greater. The basis commonly used is per tonne (1000 kilos) or per cubic metre. *See* freight ton.

ship's papers, documents that are carried by a ship (log book, certificate of registry, charter agreement, manifest, etc.).

ship's protest, a sworn statement made by a ship's master and crew stating how a ship or its cargo came to be damaged.

ship's report, a document submitted on arrival at a port by the ship's master giving details of the ship, it's crew, passengers, cargo, and voyage.

shop, a building in which goods are sold to the general public. The goods are normally on display.

shop assistant, an employee in a shop who gives advice and information to the customer on the goods offered for sale and completes the sale on behalf of the shopowner.

shoplifting, stealing goods from shops during hours of trading.

shopping centre, 1. the part of a town or city in which most of the shops are located. **2.** a specially designed area, building, etc., in which a number of different shops are located. It enables shoppers to buy all of their requirements in one visit.

short bill, a *bill of exchange that must be paid on presentation or within a stated period not exceeding ten days.

short-dated gilt, a *gilt-edged security that is redeemable within five years.

short delivery, a delivery of goods that does not agree with the *delivery note, being short in the weight, quantity, or number of items delivered.

shorthand, an abbreviated and fast form of writing or taking notes using symbols to represent words or groups of words.

shorthand typist, a person trained to write shorthand notes of letters, speeches, etc., and to type them later. *Compare* copy typist, audio-typist.

short interest, the amount by which the value of goods falls below the value for which they have been insured.

shorts, 1. short for *short-dated gilts. **2.** goods or securities sold but not bought. *See* short selling.

short selling, selling goods or securities that are not yet owned in the hope of buying them in at a lower price before the delivery date, thus making a profit.

short-term capital, money borrowed by a business for a short period, e.g. a bank overdraft. *Compare* long-term capital.

short-term deposits, money deposited with a bank, building societies, etc., that can be withdrawn at short notice.

short-term rate of interest, the rate of interest *charged on loans repayable in up to three months.

short ton, a unit of weight equal to 2000 lbs, used especially in the U.S.

show of hands, a method of voting by raising the hand, each vote carrying equal weight.

shut-down point, the level of output below which a producer is unable to cover his *direct costs, and must therefore cease production.

side deals, business deals made by company employees for private gain rather than the company's profit.

sight bill, a *bill of exchange payable on presentation.

signature, a person's name, handwritten by that person, as on cheques, letters, etc.

simple interest, a rate of interest calculated at set times on the capital sum only and not on the accumulated interest, e.g. an interest rate of 10% on £100 would produce £110 after one year, £120 after two years, etc. *Compare* compound interest.

single-life pension, a pension that is paid only to the beneficiary and not to a widow or widower after the beneficiary's death. *Compare* joint life and last survivor pensions.

single-tax system, a method of raising the entire revenue of a state by one single tax.

sinking fund, an investment fund set up to provide a specified amount of money for a particular purpose when needed.

sister-ship clause, a clause in *marine insurance policies to protect the shipowner in the event of two of his ships colliding.

sit-down strike, a strike in which workers occupy their workplace but refuse to work.

SI units, abbreviation for Système International d'Unités. The internationally agreed system of units now in use for scientific and some technological purposes. The seven basic units of the system include the kilogram, metre, second, ampere, and kelvin. The derived units include the watt, joule, volt, ohm, and hertz. The same decimal multiples are used with all units.

sleeping partner, a member of a *partnership who takes little active part in the running of the firm. Compare active partner.

sliding peg. See crawling peg.

sliding scale, a scale of charges that increase as the value of the transaction increases.

slump, an economic *depression, often one in a particular industry in which demand has fallen.

smuggling, taking goods into or out of a country illegally, either because they are banned or to avoid paying customs duty.

snake, the European Economic Community's currency arrangement in which the currencies of member states are fixed in relation to each other but float against the currencies of non-member states.

social wealth, all the assets of a country used directly (land, machines, etc.) and indirectly (hospitals, roads, etc.) in the production of goods and services.

soft currency, a currency that is in greater supply than demand in the world's foreign exchange markets. Compare hard currency.

soft loan, a loan with a very low rate of interest, often used as a form of international aid.

soft sell, selling by gentle persuasion. Compare hard sell.

software, the programs that control the operation of a *computer. Compare hardware.

sold ledger, a book kept by a business for recording all the sales made by the business.

sold note, a contract note issued by a stockbroker or commodity broker as legal evidence of a transaction in which he has sold shares or goods for his client's account. It gives the details of the sale, commission, and date of payment.

sole agent. See agent.

solicitor, a person trained in law whose job involves drawing up legal documents, giving legal advice, and acting on his client's behalf in legal disputes. A solicitor does not plead in the higher courts but he briefs the *barrister who does so.

solicitor's letter, a letter from a solicitor requesting payment of a debt owed to his client. Such a letter is written prior to taking legal action.

solo, a single copy of a *bill of exchange.

solvent, having enough money to pay outstanding debts. Compare insolvent.

special crossing, a crossing on a cheque making it payable only to the person or bank named.

special resolution, a resolution passed by the shareholders at a general meeting of a company to make some specific major change in the company, e.g. changing its name.

specific charge, a security over specific assets of a company that has borrowed money, rather than over all the assets. Compare floating charge.

sterling area

specific damages, *damages ordered by a court to be paid by one person to another when the loss suffered by the injured party can be calculated exactly. *Compare* general damages.

speculator, 1. a person who buys and sells securities, currency, or commodities in the hope of making money as a result of price movements. 2. a person who risks money in order to earn large profits.

spot currency market, the foreign-exchange market dealing in currencies for immediate delivery.

spot goods, commodities that are offered for sale for immediate delivery. *Compare* futures.

stag, a *speculator on a stock exchange who attempts to make profits by buying *new issues of shares at the issue price and selling them at a premium when stock-exchange dealings begin.

stale bull, a dealer on a stock exchange or commodity market who has a *paper profit on securities or goods bought but is unable to realize this profit as there are insufficient buyers.

stale cheque, a cheque that has become out of date, usually six months after issue.

stamp duty, a tax on certain legal transactions, in which a stamp is attached to the documents.

standard of living, the level of prosperity a person or society enjoys, in terms of material and social benefits, e.g. food, housing, etc.

standard rate, the basic rate of income tax paid on earnings, after the deduction of allowances.

stand-by agreement, an agreement under which a member country of the *International Monetary Fund can make an immediate withdrawal of money.

standing order, an order given to one's bank to pay a specified sum to a specified person or organization at regular intervals.

starboard, the right hand side of ship (facing forward).

state bank, a U.S. commercial bank that has a state charter, rather than a federal charter, and is controlled by state laws.

state lottery, a lottery in which the proceeds, after paying prizes and expenses, are kept by the state.

statement, a document that gives details of one person's or company's account with another. It lists invoices and payments for the period and shows the amount outstanding.

state ownership, ownership by the state of certain or all of a country's means of production.

state planning, the guidance of nation's economic activities by the government.

statute law, law enacted by parliament as opposed to common law.

statutes of limitation, laws that fix the time limit after which legal action cannot be taken.

statutory books, the records that limited companies are required by U.K. law to keep. These include a register of directors, a register of shareholders, and account books.

statutory company, a company set up by an Act of Parliament.

statutory meeting, a shareholders' meeting that limited companies are required by law to hold within three months of the start of business.

statutory report, a detailed report on a company that its directors must send to the shareholders prior to the *statutory meeting.

sterling area, those countries that have officially linked their curren-

sterling balances

cies to sterling. They are known officially as the scheduled territories.

sterling balances, sterling held by foreign governments and commercial interests, which represent a major part of the U.K.'s reserves.

stock, 1. fixed interest securities or government loans. 2. ordinary shares. 3. (stock-in trade) the total quantity of goods held by a company, comprising completed products, work-in-progress, component parts, and raw materials. In the U.S. the word *inventory is usually used.

stockbroker, a person who offers investment advice and buys and sells securities on a *stock exchange on behalf of his clients. He charges a commission for this service.

stock exchange, a market in which stocks and shares can be bought and sold. The world's largest stock exchanges are in New York, London, and Tokyo.

stock-in-trade. *See* stock.

stockjobber, a member of the London Stock Exchange who deals in stocks and shares. He does not trade directly with the public but deals with them through a *stockbroker. He makes his profit by selling at a higher price than the price at which he buys.

stockpiling, building up reserves of materials for use in a shortage or national emergency.

stocktaking, checking and listing the quantity of *stock held by a company or other organization.

stop-go, government economic policy in the form of alternating inflationary and deflationary measures in an attempt to keep in phase with the recessions and booms of the business cycle.

stop-loss order, an instruction given to a stockbroker or commodity broker by his client to sell a particular holding if its price falls to a stated level.

stoppage in transitu, taking over goods or commercial documents while they are in transit to a buyer who has not paid for them and who has become insolvent.

stowage plan, a plan of the cargo space on a particular ship showing where each lot of cargo is stowed.

strike, a stoppage of work by employees to force their employers into some course of action, often increasing wages.

strong room, a room, usually fireproof and burglar-proof, in which money or other valuables are stored for safe keeping.

sub-agent, an agent who acts for another agent rather than a *principal.

sub-lease, a lease of land granted by a leaseholder rather than by the freeholder of the land.

subpoena, a court order instructing a person to appear in court at a specified time.

subrogation, the right of an insurer to take over from a person whose claim he has paid any rights relating to the subject of the loss, e.g. claims on a third party.

subscribed. *See* issued capital.

subscriber, 1. a person who signs a company's *memorandum of association; the subscribers appoint the company's first directors. 2. a person who pays money regularly in order to receive a publication.

subscription shares, shares in a company that are paid for in instalments, e.g. building society shares.

subsidiary, a company that is controlled by another company, either through its directors or because more than half its shares

systems analysis

are owned by the controlling company.

subsidy, money paid by the government to certain producers, e.g. farmers, in order to keep the price of the product below its market price or to keep the producers in business.

subsistence level, the minimum standard of living for survival.

subsistence wage, the lowest wage rate at which it is possible to survive.

substantial damage, damages awarded in a civil case to the person bringing the action. They are usually sufficiently high to compensate for the loss sustained.

supermarket, a self-service shop, usually selling food, drink, and a number of other items, including household goods and clothes.

supplementary benefits, payments made by the U.K. government to assist those in special need, e.g. the unemployed, pensioners and families below a certain income level.

supplier, a person or company that provides goods or services directly to a buyer.

supply and demand, the market forces that in a free-enterprise system determine the price of a product or service. When supply exceeds demand prices tend to fall when demand exceeds supply prices tend to rise.

surety, a *guarantee usually in the form of money.

surrender value, the amount of money that can be claimed by the holder of certain types of life-assurance policies when the policy is cancelled before maturity.

switching, the transfer of invested money from one type of security to another.

sympathetic strike, a strike by workers not directly involved in a dispute in support of another group of workers who are on strike.

syndicate, a group consisting of invidual businessmen or businesses working together for their common benefit.

systems analysis, the study and design of the methods and techniques of using a computer for a specific purpose.

T

tacit agreement, an agreement that is implied rather than formally stated.

takehome pay, the earnings that a person receives from an employment after all deductions, such as tax, insurance, etc.

takeover bid, an offer made by one company to the shareholders of another to purchase their shares and thus gain control of the company. Bids are often successful even when the board of directors is opposed to the move. To gain control the buyers need to purchase at least 51% of the company's voting shares.

tallyman, a person who checks that the cargo unloaded from a ship agrees with the listed details of the cargo.

talon, a slip of paper attached to a *bearer bond; it is used to apply for a new sheet of dividend coupons.

tangible assets, the principal assets of a company (property, machinery, etc.), not including unsold stock. Compare intangible assets.

tap stocks, government *gilt-edged securities that are available for purchase when their market price reaches a certain figure.

tare, the weight of a container in which goods are transported or the weight of the carrying vehicle. For example, the tare of a road vehicle is deducted from the *gross weight as shown by a *weighbridge to give the *nett weight of the goods carried.

tariff, 1. a government import tax on certain specified goods making them more expensive in the importing country. It is often imposed to protect a domestic industry. **2.** a list of itemized charges, as in a hotel.

tax, a compulsory payment levied by the government on income, property, financial transactions, etc. See income tax, corporation tax, capital transfer tax, value added tax, capital gains tax.

taxable income, a person's income on which his liability for tax is assessed. It is equal to his *gross income less allowable expenses and outgoings and less certain personal *allowances. See also nett income.

taxation, the raising of government revenue either directly (e.g. income tax) or indirectly (e.g. value-added tax). It is used to finance government expenditure and as a means of implementing economic policy.

tax avoidance, legal means of keeping the amount of tax payable to a minimum. Compare tax evasion.

tax base, the basis for assessing a particular tax liability, e.g. *taxable income for income tax.

tax collector. See collector of taxes.

tax-deductible, denoting expenses insured in running a business or doing a job that can be set against a liability for tax.

tax evasion, the illegal non-payment of taxes by submitting false information or not declaring income or revenue to the tax authorities. Compare tax avoidance.

tax haven, a country that has low taxes and is therefore attractive to foreigners or to companies who may wish to open offices there.

tax inspector. See inspector of taxes.

tax loss, a capital loss that can be set against a capital gain for assessment of *capital gains tax.

tax relief, a reduction in the liability for tax of a person or company in certain circumstances, e.g. on income tax when part of the income has been spent on a mortgage or on certain types of machinery.

tax year. *See* financial year.

technical rally, a rise in prices on a stock market or a commodity market resulting from a shortage of stocks or a shortage of goods.

telegraphic address, an identifying word used, instead of the full name and address of a company, in telegrams and cables. It provides a saving in the cost of sending a telegram when the charge is based on the number of words.

telegraphic transfers, a method of transferring money quickly through a bank to other countries using cabled instructions to the foreign bank.

telephone credit card, a credit card issued by a post office enabling the holder to make calls through the operator from any telephone and to have the cost charged to his account.

telephone directory, a post office publication listing telephone subscribers' names, addresses, and telephone numbers in alphabetical order.

teleprinter, a device, with a keyboard similar to a typewriter, used to send and receive messages by *Telex.

Telex, an international post office service enabling messages to be sent direct from one subscriber to another. The messages are sent by typing them on a *teleprinter and are received on the same instrument. Subscribers are called up by dial.

teller, a bank employee who handles withdrawals and deposits of money by the bank's clients.

tender, an offer to supply goods or services at a stated price on stated conditions in response to an invitation from the buyer to submit an offer.

tenor, the period between the date of receipt of a *bill of exchange and the date on which it is payable.

term assurance, a type of life assurance in which payment is made only if the assured dies within a period specified.

term bill, a *bill of exchange that becomes payable on a specified day rather than on demand.

terminal market, a *commodity market dealing in *futures that is sited close to the users rather than to the producers.

territorial waters, the part of the sea adjoining the coastline of a country over which it claims sovereignty. It usually extends to a limit of three miles.

third-party insurance, an insurance policy that covers loss to a person or company other than the insurer or the insured.

Third World, the developing countries as opposed to the industrialized nations.

threshold agreement, an agreement that entitles employees to a wage increase if the inflation rate exceeds a specified level.

tied loan, a loan by one country to another with the stipulation that the money will be spent with the country providing the loan. On this basis it provides benefit to both countries.

time and motion study, a study of the time taken and the method used by a worker or workers to do a particular task. *See also* work study.

timecard, a card that records the times at which a worker starts and

time charter

finishes work. It is used to calculate his wages.

time charter. See chartering.

tip, a sum of money voluntarily given by a customer to a waiter, bar attendant, etc., in addition to the bill. See also service charge.

title, right of ownership to particular goods, property, etc.

title deed, a legal document providing proof of ownership of a particular piece of land.

token coin, a coin that is worth more as money than for its metal content. Most coinage now consists of token coins.

toll, a charge made for using certain roads, bridges, or tunnels.

ton, a unit of weight equal to 20 hundredweight or 2240 lbs (*long ton*). A *short ton*, often used in the U.S., is equal to 2000 lbs or 20 short hundredweight of 100 lbs each. See also shipping ton, tonne.

tonnage. See deadweight tonnage, displacement tonnage, measurement tonnage.

tonnage deck, a ship's upper deck if it has less than three decks, or the second from below if it has three or more.

tonne, a *metric ton of 1000 kilograms.

top-hat scheme, a pension scheme for the senior executives of a company, especially one in which the company pays the premiums.

tort, a civil offence, such as negligence, deceit, defamation, etc., arising from a failure to carry out one's obligations. Court action may result from a tort but it does not include criminal offences or breach of contract.

total income, a person's income before deduction of allowances for tax purposes. See also gross income.

towage, the amount charged for towing a ship by tug into or out of a harbour.

town gas, gas manufactured from coal for use as a domestic and industrial fuel. See also natural gas.

toxic waste, any poisonous waste material that arises from an industrial process.

trade account, a credit account at a shop or supplier for customers in a particular trade. For example, a building contractor will have a trade account with a builders' merchant.

trade advertising, advertising directed at a particular industry or profession rather than the general public.

trade association, an association of traders in the same field, formed for their mutual benefit.

trade barrier, any government restrictions, such as tariffs, quotas, etc., to control imports into a country.

trade bill, a *bill of exchange drawn on a trader and usually commanding a lower discount rate than a *bank bill.

trade bloc, an association of countries formed to encourage trade between them.

trade creditor, a company or individual who is owed money for goods or services supplied.

trade cycle (business cycle), the fluctuations that a country's economy undergoes. A *boom is followed by a *recession, leading to a *depression. The *recovery from the depression leads to another boom.

trade directory, a publication giving the names and addresses of companies operating in a particular field.

trade discount, a reduction in the normal selling price of goods given to a person or firm who will resell the goods or who will use them in the course of business. For example, one antique dealer will give a trade discount to another and a supplier of car parts will often give a discount to a motor repairer.

trade fair, an exhibition of the products of a particular industry attended principally by traders rather than by the general public.

trade gap, the amount by which the value of a country's imports exceeds the value of its exports.

trade investments, investments made by a company to protect and further its business; for example, a company may invest in a company from whom it buys components in order to protect its source of supply.

trademark, the motif or identifying symbol by which a company or its products are known. *See also* tradename.

tradename, the name under which a company sells and advertises a product or series of products. Tradenames, like trademarks, can be registered to stop other companies using the same, or similar, names or marks.

trade reference, a reference regarding the creditworthiness of a company or business. For example, a retailer wanting to open a credit account with a wholesaler would normally give the names of at least two companies he deals with as references.

trade tests, tests of a tradesman's (or apprentice's) skill. They ensure that the tradesman is capable of a standard of work that qualifies him to practise his trade or craft.

trade union, an association of workers formed to safeguard their interests in negotiations with employees. *See also* craft union, industrial union, general union.

trading bank, an Australian commercial bank.

trading estate. *See* industrial estate.

trading stamps, stamps bought by retail shops, garages, etc., and issued free to their customers with goods purchased. When the customer has collected enough stamps he exchanges them for goods from the trading stamp company.

tramp, a cargo ship that can be hired to carry cargo between any ports. Unlike a *liner it does not run on a scheduled route.

transaction, any commercial deal.

transfer-charge call, a telephone call made through the operator, in which the cost of the call is charged to the account of the number being called, provided that the subscriber accepts the call on these terms.

transfer deed, a document proving the transfer of land, securities, etc., from one person to another.

transferee, the person to whom something is transferred.

transfer form, a document signed by the seller of securities in order to effect the transfer of the securities to the purchaser and to record the transfer in the company's register of shareholders.

transhipment, the transference of goods from one ship to another. It may be required because there is no direct connection between the port of shipment and the destination, or for some political reason.

transport, 1. the carrying of people or goods from one place to another. **2.** the vehicle used.

travel agent, a person or company acting on behalf of airlines, railways, shipping companies, and holiday tour operators in selling of tickets and holidays to members of the public or to companies.

travellers' cheques, cheques issued by a bank for use when travelling abroad. They can be changed into

travelling expenses

foreign currency as required. They usually have two spaces for the payee's signature, one signature being added on issue and the other in the presence of the paying bank.

travelling expenses, expenses incurred in the course of travel on business.

Treasury, the U.K. government body, under the direction of the Chancellor of the Exchequer, that is responsible for the country's financial and economic affairs.

Treasury bill, a short-term government security, usually enabling the government to borrow money for three months at a low rate of interest.

Treasury stocks, gilt-edged securities issued by the U.K. Treasury, rates of interest varying with the redemption date. For example, a 9% Treasury stock (1994) pays 9% interest and is redeemable at par in 1994.

trial balance, an accounting procedure to ensure that the books of account are accurate. It involves checking that the sum of the credits is equal to the sum of the debits.

troy weight, a system of units of weight for gold, silver, and precious stones. One troy pound (0·373 kg or 0·82 of an *avoirdupois pound) consists of 12 troy ounces, 240 pennyweights, or 5760 grains.

trust, 1. money or property held by a *trustee or trustees on behalf of a person. **2.** (in the U.S.) a number of companies that have merged their interests to form a *cartel. In the U.S., anti-trust laws seek to prevent such mergers.

trust companies, a company formed in order to act as a trustee or to carry out the business of a trust.

trust deed, a document that sets out the conditions and terms of a *trust and transfers the property covered by the trust to named trustees.

trustee, a person who holds and administers money or property in *trust on behalf of another person (the beneficiary). Although the trustee or trustees are the owners of the property for the duration of the trust, their management of it is strictly regulated by law.

trustee in bankruptcy, a person appointed to deal with the property of a bankrupt for the benefit of the creditors. *See also* official receiver.

trustee investments, investments of money, securities, property, etc., held by *trustees on behalf of a *trust. *See also* trustee securities.

trustee securities, securities of a sufficiently stable nature to be held by *trustees and paid for by *trust funds. If the *trust deed does not specify how the money is to be invested, the trustees must invest only in those securities sanctioned by law as suitable for trust funds.

trust fund, the fund of money or property held in *trust for a person by *trustees. The investment of the fund is at the discretion of the trustees, subject to whatever is said in the *trust deed and certain legal provisions. *See* trustee securities.

tug, a small boat used to tow larger vessels, usually into and out of a harbour.

turnover, the value of a company's total annual sales.

tycoon, a businessman who has made a great deal of money through his activities.

typescript, a typed copy of a document, book, manuscript, etc.

typist, a person who operates a typewriter, especially a person in an office who does so as an occupation.

U

uberrima fides. *See* utmost good faith.

ullage, 1. the amount of space unfilled in a barrel, tank, or other vessel. *See also* vacuity. **2.** (in Customs terminology) the actual contents of such a container.

ultimo, of the previous month. Often abbreviated to *ult*. E.g. 24th ult. refers to the 24th of last month. *Compare* instant, proximo.

ultra vires, denoting an action that goes beyond the legal powers of the person or company taking the action.

umpire, a person in an *arbitration who makes the final ruling if the arbitrators are unable to agree. He is usually selected by the abitrators before the arbitration takes place.

unabsorbed costs, the portion of the *indirect costs (rent, rates, etc.) of an undertaking that is not absorbed as a result of a failure to meet production targets. For example, a company producing doors and allocating £1 per door to cover indirect costs on a target of 20,000 doors would have a fund of £20,000 to meet indirect costs. However, if they only made 18,000 doors in the period, they would have unabsorbed costs of £2000.

uncalled capital, the portion of the capital to be raised by an issue of shares that is not payable by shareholders when the shares are issued. *Compare* called-up capital.

unconfirmed letter of credit, a *letter of credit that does not have the guarantee of payment by the negotiating bank should the issuing bank fail to pay. *Compare* confirmed letter of credit.

unconstitutional strike, a strike that breaks agreed procedures for industrial action laid down by a *trade union.

UNCTAD. *See* United Nations Conference on Trade and Development.

undated securities. *See* irredeemable security.

under-deck tonnage, a measure of the cargo-carrying capacity of a ship, expressed as the *measurement tonnage up to the *tonnage deck.

under separate cover, sent in a separate package or envelope.

undersubscription, a situation that arises when not all the shares offered in a *new issue are bought.

underwriter, 1. an official appointed by an insurance company to decide whether or not to accept specific insurance risks. *See also* Lloyd's underwriter. **2.** a person or company that agrees to buy a certain proportion of a *new issue of shares from a company if they are not taken up by the public.

underwriting syndicate. *See* Lloyd's underwriter.

undischarged bankrupt, a person who has been declared bankrupt and has not paid off his debts and received a discharge from the court. Undischarged bankrupts are barred from holding many public offices, managerial posts, and from borrowing without informing their creditors.

undisclosed principal, a person who transacts business through an agent or broker on the understanding that his name will not be disclosed. The agent or broker must always make it

undistributed profits

clear when he is acting for an undisclosed principal.

undistributed profits, profits that are not distributed to shareholders as dividends but are retained by the company for capital investment, etc.

undue influence, pressure on an individual to sign a contract that he might not have otherwise have signed. Contracts made under undue influence will not be enforced by the courts.

unearned income, money obtained from investments, property, etc., rather than from paid employment. Unearned income is taxed at a higher rate than earned income in some countries.

unemployables, people who cannot find work even in times of full employment, usually because of poor health or some other handicap. *See also* residual unemployment.

unemployment, the proportion of the workforce in a particular country or region that is unable to find work.

unemployment benefit, regular payments made by the state to those who are unemployed.

unfair trade practice, a method of carrying on business that does not comply with accepted codes of business conduct or with government legislation.

unilateral, one-sided; carried out by only one party to a contract, agreement, etc.

unissued capital, the amount of a company's capital that is not in the form of shares issued to shareholders.

unit cost, the total cost of manufacturing a number of units of a product, divided by the number of units. *Also called* average cost.

United Nations Conference on Trade and Development (UNCTAD), a United Nations agency to promote the international trade problems of the *developing countries.

unit trust, an investment trust that buys securities in large quantities, selling shares (units) of the total holding to the public. Dividends are pooled and shared amongst the unitholders. Usually a bank or insurance company acts as trustee. Some unit trusts specialize in securities with a high yield, others specialize in securities that can be expected to give substantial capital gains.

Universal Postal Union (U.P.U.), a United Nations agency that controls the international postage service.

unlimited company, a company whose owners (shareholders) are jointly liable for the company's debts up to the limit of their personal resources.

unliquidated damages, compensation resulting from a breach of contract, the amount of the compensation not being stated in the contract. Damages in this case have to be decided by a court. *Compare* liquidated damages.

unofficial strike, a strike carried out by members of a trade union without the consent of their union leaders.

unpaid services, services, such as housework, for which no payment is made and which are therefore excluded from calculations of the national product.

unquoted securities, shares, etc. that are not dealt in on a *stock exchange.

unsecured creditor, a creditor of a bankrupt or a company undergoing liquidation whose claim is not secured against property of the debtor. Unsecured creditors are paid after *secured creditors and after taxes, wages, etc., have been paid.

unsecured debenture, a debenture that is not secured against the

utmost good faith

property or assets of a company. If payment is not made when it is due unsecured debenture-holders must wait for payment until the company has been wound up.

U.P.U. *See* Universal Postal Union.

usance, the time customarily allowed, usually 60 days, for the payment of *bills of exchange between foreign countries.

U.S. customary units, the U.S. system of units based on Imperial units. The principal differences between U.S. units and Imperial units are the gallon (1 U.S. gallon = 0·8327 Imperial gallons) and the ton (1 U.S. ton = 2000 lbs).

usufract, the right to use another person's property without damaging it or lowering its value.

usury, lending money at exorbitant rates of interest.

utilities, services such as water, electricity, etc., provided for the public, usually by government agencies.

utility company, a company, such as a water works, providing a basic service for the general public.

utmost good faith, a legal obligation by both parties to an insurance contract to reveal to each other any information that might affect either's decision to make to the contract. Failure to do so can make the contract void.

V

vacuity, (in Customs terminology) the amount of space unfilled in a barrel, tank, or other vessel; ullage.

valid, legally acceptable; not expired.

valuation, an estimate of the value of goods, property, etc., at current market rates.

value added tax (VAT), a form of indirect taxation in which a tax is charged on the value added to goods at each stage of production; the amount paid in VAT by each producer is repaid to him by the government, so that the final tax falls entirely on the consumer.

value in use, the usefulness of an item to its user as opposed to its market value.

VAT. *See* value added tax.

vending machine, a machine that dispenses goods automatically when the required amount of money is inserted.

vendor, the seller in a transaction.

venture capital. *See* risk capital.

vertical integration, the merger of various companies involved in different stages of production of a particular product. *Compare* horizontal integration.

vertical mobility, the extent to which people can change jobs involving a change in status. *Compare* horizontal mobility.

vested interest, 1. a stake (often financial) in the continuance or outcome of something, e.g. landowners have a vested interest in opposing land tax. **2.** a legal right or title to goods or land held securely in the possession of the owner.

vice-chairman, the position immediately below that of *chairman.

vintner, a person dealing in wine.

visa, a document required, in addition to a passport, for entry into certain countries. Application for a visa must be made to the embassy of the country to be visited.

visibles, items of international trade that are tangible goods as opposed to services. The *balance of trade includes only visibles. *Compare* invisibles.

vocational guidance, professional advice in deciding on a person's choice of job.

vocational training, training for a specific job or career.

void, 1. not enforceable by law. **2.** empty.

voluntary liquidation, the closing down of a company because it cannot pay its debts. A member's voluntary liquidation results from a decision of the members of the company to wind up the company. A creditor's voluntary liquidation is organized by the company's creditors, who appoint the *liquidator.

vostro account, a bank account in a particular country held by a foreign bank. *Compare* nostro account.

voting rights, the right of *ordinary shareholders to vote as stated in a company's *prospectus.

voting shares, shares that entitle their owners to vote at the company's annual general meeting or at extraordinary meetings. They are usually *ordinary shares.

voucher, 1. a document that can be exchanged for goods or for money.

2. a document, receipt, etc., that proves that money has been received or paid as stated in a book of account.

voyage charter. *See* chartering.

voyage policy, a *marine insurance policy covering cargo and ship for a particular voyage.

W

W.A. *Abbreviation for* with average.

wage claim, a claim by workers, often members of a *trade union, for a rise or variation in their rates of pay.

wage differential, 1. the difference in wage rates earned by one type of tradesman or worker compared with another type. **2.** the difference in wage rates paid in different parts of the country for the same kind of work.

wage-earner, a person who is paid an hourly or weekly wage for work done.

wage-freeze, a policy adopted by a government to control *inflation; employers are not allowed to raise wages beyond stated limits for a stated period.

wage-price spiral, an *inflationary spiral in which increasing wages cause increasing costs to industry, which in turn is obliged to raise prices for its products. Increased prices then lead to further demands for increased wages, and so on.

wage rates, payment made for work done either on a time basis, or on an output basis.

wage restraint, a form of voluntary *wage freeze.

wages agreement, an agreement reached between two or more parties (usually a *trade union and an employer, although the government may be involved) that settles outstanding questions regarding future wage rates.

waiver, a voluntary agreement to give up a legal right, often to ignore the benefits of a specific clause in a contract.

warehouse, a building for storing goods. *See also* bonded warehouse, public warehouse.

warehouse officer, a Customs officer who inspects goods entering and leaving a *bonded warehouse.

warehousing, 1. the storing of goods in a *warehouse. **2.** the anonymous purchase of small blocks of shares through *nominees until the true owner has a sufficiently large interest in the company concerned to make a *take-over bid for it.

warrant, a document issued by a *public warehouse that gives details of goods stored in the warehouse. The person named on the warrant is entitled to remove the goods on presentation of the warrant, which is, therefore, a negotiable document. *Also called:* warehouse warrant, wharfinger's warrant.

warranty, a guarantee that a manufactured article is free of defects and that any parts found to be faulty will be replaced free of charge.

war risk insurance, a type of insurance that covers risks arising from war between nations. In *cargo insurance the risks covered are usually those laid down by the Institute of London Underwriters.

waste products, products left over from a manufacturing process that are of no value. Some can be easily disposed of but others, such as radioactive waste products, present great problems.

wasting asset, an asset, such as an oil-field, that has a limited life lasting only until the deposits of oil are extracted and used up.

water damage, damage to goods caused by water. Fresh-water damage may occur during transit by river or canal or during a fire. *Seawater damage is usually more serious.

waybill, a list of goods sent by some form of transport. *See also* air waybill.

wear and tear, the accepted deterioration in a product or a building through use.

weather insurance. *See* pluvial insurance.

weather working days, the number of days on which a vessel can load or unload in a port, weather permitting, without incurring charges. *See also* lay days.

weighted average, an arithmetic average that takes into account the relative importance of some external criterion. For example, if a company employs five people, the two heads of the company earning £10,000 p.a. each and three employees each earning £3000 p.a., the simple average earnings would be (10,000 + 3000)/2 = £6500 p.a. A more reliable guide would be the weighted average calculated: (3000 × 3/5) + (10,000 × 2/5) = £5800 p.a.

weight note, 1. a note issued by a seller of goods to the buyer listing the weights of all packages delivered. **2.** a similar note issued by a *public warehouse when goods are imported into a country.

weight or measurement (W/M), a method of quoting *freight rates for cargo on ships. The rate is quoted per 1000 kilograms or per cubic metre, whichever is the greater.

welfare state, a country that provides comprehensive social benefits for people, including a health service, sickness benefits, unemployment pay, etc.

wharf, a quay or pier, often with *warehouses, alongside which ships can be moored for the purpose of loading or unloading cargo.

wharfage, a charge made for the use of a *wharf.

wharfinger, a person who owns or is in charge of a *wharf.

wharfinger's receipt, a receipt issued by a wharfinger for cargo received at a wharf for shipment overseas.

wharfinger's warrant. *See* warrant.

white-collar worker, a person who works in an office and is engaged in clerical, administrative, or managerial duties.

whole-life insurance, an assurance policy that is payable only on the death of the assured.

wholesale price, the price of a product as sold in large quantities to a *retailer.

wholesaler, a person engaged in the sale of goods in large quantities to *retailers, rather than direct to consumers.

wildcat strike, a strike that is arranged quickly and does not have trade-union approval.

windfall, an unexpected piece of good fortune, especially a unexpected payment or sum of money received or inherited by a person.

winding-up, the process of dissolving a company, usually following *bankruptcy.

windmill. *See* accommodation bill.

window envelope, an envelope with a transparent panel through which the addressee's name and address can be seen printed on the enclosure.

with average (W.A.), *cargo insurance terms that cover all *free of particular average risks and also the

without prejudice

risk of damage or partial loss by sea water or heavy weather.

without prejudice, a qualification implying that a statement made has no legal force and cannot be used as evidence in a court of law.

without recourse (sans recours), an endorsement on a *bill of exchange indicating that the holder cannot obtain compensation from the person from whom he bought it.

with-profits policy, a life-assurance policy that entitles the holder to a share of the profits earned by the company issuing the policy. The premiums are usually higher than an equivalent without-profits policy.

witness, 1. a person who gives evidence in a court of law. **2.** a person who verifies the genuineness of a signature or a document by adding his own signature.

workers' participation, the participation by workers in the management and profits of the companies for which they work.

work force, the total number of workers employed by a company, factory, or industry.

work-in, a form of *industrial action by workers in which they continue to work and refuse to leave their place of work in order to avoid being locked out by their employer.

working capital, the difference between the current *assets and the current *liabilities of a company, which is available for the general furtherance of the business.

working conditions, the conditions under which the employees of a company are expected to work. It includes the safety precautions, the hours worked, the provisions made for rest periods and refreshment, the washing facilities, etc.

working days, the days on which work is carried out. Normal working days exclude Sundays and public holidays. *Compare* running days.

working expenses, the costs of running a business, such as wages and salaries, rent, overheads, etc. In a *profit and loss account they are deducted from the *gross profit in order to arrive at the *nett profit.

working partner, a partner in a firm who works full-time for the firm. *Compare* sleeping partner, active partner.

working to rule, a form of *industrial action that puts pressure on the management of a company in order to gain some end in favour of the workers, without going on strike. The workers obey all the rules meticulously with the result that production is slowed down.

working week, the number of hours worked each week by a worker.

work-in-progress, the value, at a specified date, of work that has been started but not completed. This figure is usually included in the *balance sheet and *profit and loss account of a business.

work permit, a permit issued by a government agency of a country authorizing a foreigner to work or to seek work in that country.

work study, an examination of the way a particular job is done in order to find the most efficient methods of doing it in terms of both time and effort.

World Bank Group, an international bank originally set up in 1946 as the International Bank for Reconstruction and Development to assist in the economic recovery of all nations after World War II, especially the *developing countries. Two other organizations were later added to form the group: the International Finance Corporation, to assist private investors, and the Inter-

written-down value

national Development Association, to provide loans to developing countries.

writ, an order issued by a court or other authority requiring the person upon whom it is served to do or refrain from doing some specified act, or to appear in court on a certain date.

write off, 1. to delete items from an inventory of stocks when they are no longer serviceable or useful. **2.** to remove an amount from the debt of a company when it becomes clear that the amount will never be recovered, e.g. owing to the bankruptcy of the debtor.

written-down value, the value of an asset of a company after deducting *depreciation.

X, Y, Z

Xerox, a copy of a document, letter, etc., obtained by a dry process (xerography) in which a coloured powder adheres to parts of a paper surface that are electrically charged.

yearling bond, a *bond that is intended to be repaid after one year.

yield, the income from an investment expressed as a percentage of its current market value. A £1-share paying 20p per share and having a market value of £2.50 is yielding 8%. This is the current (or flat) yield. *See also* redemption yield.

yield gap, the difference between the average *yield on ordinary shares and that on government securities.

zipcode, the postal code added to addresses to facilitate sorting and distribution of mail by the Post Office.